The Best Advice You'll Ever Get!

An A-Z Guide

by

Aubrey Malone

Introduction

We only ask for advice when we've already made up our minds – right? The people we revere, i.e. the ones who give us 'good' advice, are the ones who tell us what we want to hear. For example, 'I'm thinking of dumping Bob. What do you think?' 'I agree!' That's a friend. Example 2: 'I'm thinking of dumping Bob. What would you advise?' 'I wouldn't rush into anything.' 'Thanks. You're a great help. Byee!'

Logan Pearsall Smith said, 'Don't tell your friends their faults. It might cure them but they'll never forgive you.' Terry Prachett added, 'When you seek advice from someone, it's certainly not because you want them to give it. You just want them to be there while you talk to yourself.' .

My favourite word of advice came from George Bernard Shaw. He said, 'Never take anyone's advice.'

So now you don't have to read this book.

A

Aardvarks

Never let an aardvark near your cocaine. (David Corrado)

Abortion

Don't knock aborted children. They're very well behaved. Busy parents should take account of that. They're also less expensive to raise. Very few abortions ever go to college, for instance, though one would not necessarily know this from touring a campus. (P.J. O'Rourke)

Accidents

Avoid road accidents. Drive on the pavement. (Les Dawson)

75% of road accidents occur within five minutes of home. Move house. (Russell Harty)

Achievement

There are three ways to get something done. Do it yourself, have someone else do it or forbid your kids to do it. (Minta Crane)

Acne

If a serial killer is pointing a gun at your forehead, this may not be the best time to tell him he has acne. (Mark Greene)

Acquaintances

Should old acquaintances be forgot? Definitely. (W. Somerset Maugham)

Acquired Tastes

Don't bother with acquired tastes. They take too long to acquire. Stick with the ones you have instead – especially if they're bad ones. (Quentin Crisp)

Acting

There are only two things you need to remember before going on stage: Wipe your nose and check your flies. (Alec Guinness)

I have a good stage tip. Avoid the edge. (Emo Philips)

Know your lines and don't bump into the furniture. (Noel Coward)

The important thing in acting is to be able to laugh and cry. If I have to cry I think about my sex life. If I have to laugh I think about my sex life. (Glenda Jackson)

Activity

Don't just do something, stand there. (Clint Eastwood)

Keep busy. Dogs never piss on moving cars. (Tom Waits)

Actors

Never work with children or animals. (David O. Selznick)

Never work with children, animals or Denholm Elliott. (Gabriel Byrne)

Never marry an actor. They perform in every room in the house except the boudoir – unless there's a mirror in there. (Brigitte Bardot

Actresses

Never marry an actress on account of they have their careers and work bad hours. (Ernest Hemingway)

I have no advice to give to young actors. To young struggling actresses my advice is to keep struggling. If you struggle long enough you'll never get into trouble. But if you never get into trouble you'll never be an actress. (Groucho Marx)

Admiration

Don't accept your dog's admiration as conclusive evidence that you're wonderful. (Ann Landers)

Advertising

Don't miss our show. Six beautiful dancing girls, five beautiful costumes. (Poster outside London nightclub)

After-Dinner Speeches

The best way to stay awake during an after-dinner speech is to give it. (Fred Metcalf)

Age

Never make the mistake of being seventy. (Casey Stengal)

Marry a man your age no matter what you look like. As your beauty fades, so will his eyesight. (Phyllis Diller)

Always behave in a manner befitting your age. For example, if you're 16 or under, try not to go bald. (Woody Allen)

After the age of 45, don't try and jump the net if you win a game. Especially if it's badminton. (Michael Green)

If you're going to lie about your age, do it in the opposite direction to the normal way. Tell people you're 97 and they'll think you look fucking brilliant. (Billy Connolly)

Agreement

Don't say yes until I've finished talking. (Darryl F. Zanuck)

Air

Help fight air pollution. Stop breathing. (Milton Berle)

Air Shows

If you've got a son, go. To the Farnborough Air Show. If you haven't, go upstairs and make one. (Jeremy Clarkson)

Airports

Avoid airport delays by becoming a pilot. With a bit of persuasion they might even allow you bring your luggage into the cockpit. (Richard Waterhouse)

Alcohol

Develop a love for alcohol. It's your enemy, but the Bible says love your enemies. (Brendan Grace)

If you want to do a deal in Hollywood, join the Beverly Hills AA. (Mary Kenny)

Alertness

Be alert. Your country needs lerts. (Jim Davidson)

Algebra

Stand firm in your refusal to remain conscious during algebra. In real life, I assure you, there is no such thing as algebra. (Fran Lebowitz)

Alimony

Don't get mad if your husband leaves you. Get everything. (Ivana Trump)

Alligators

Don't cast aspersions on the alligator's mother before you cross the stream. (Con Houlihan)

Almonds

Don't eat too many almonds. They add weight to the breasts. (Colette)

America

If you're going to America, bring your own food. (Deirdre O'Kane)

Ambition

Never burn bridges. Today's junior prick, tomorrow's senior partner. (Sigourney Weaver)

Ambulances

The health service is now in such a bad state that the pizza delivery man will probably get to your house quicker than an ambulance so here's a suggestion. The next time you get a heart attack, ring for a pizza. (Ella McSweeney)

Amnesia

Become a psychic amnesiac. You'll be able to know in advance what you're going to forget. (Michael McShane)

Forget about your amnesia. It's not a danger to your health. (Angela Sissoon)

Anger

When angry, count to ten. When very angry, swear. (Mark Twain)

Never go to bed mad. Stay up and fight. (Phyllis Diller)

Never go to bed mad. Stay up and plot your revenge. (Paul Casey)

Don't get mad, get angry. (Edwina Currie)

Animals

No animal should jump on the dining room furniture unless he's absolutely certain he can hold his own in the conversation. (Fran Lebowitz)

Anniversaries

The best way to get your husband to remember your anniversary is to get married on his birthday. (Cindy Garner)

Anonymous Letters

Any man who would stoop so low as to write an anonymous letter should have the decency to sign his name to it. (Sir Boyle Roche)

Never answer an anonymous letter. (Sydney Smith)

Anticipation

Hesitate before you leap. (Sam Goldwyn)

Don't look before you leap. It ruins the surprise. (Kris Brand)

Appetites

Don't let love interfere with your appetite. (Anthony Trollope)

The best way to sharpen your appetite is to swallow razor blades before you eat. (Janet Rogers)

Apples

Eat an apple a day. It means you can have a rare old time with the doctor's wife. (Brendan Grace)

Apples are so expensive these days, you may as well have the doctor. (Henny Youngman)

Apple Tarts

Don't upset the apple tart. (Bertie Ahern)

Archaeologists

Marry an archaeologist. The older you get, the more interested he is in you. (Agatha Christie)

Ardour

If at first you don't succeed, try a little ardour. (Nigel Rees)

Arguments

Never argue with a fool. People might not know the difference. (Arthur Bloch)

When you have no basis for an argument, abuse the plaintiff. (Marcus Cicero)

Never argue with your wife. It's just your word against hundreds of hers. (Jack Benny)

The Army

Join the army, see the world, meet interesting people – and kill them. (Bill Hicks)

Join the army and see the next world. (Spike Milligan)

Armageddon

Don't worry about the world ending today. It's already tomorrow in Australia. (Steven Wright)

Art Galleries

If you're visiting a popular art gallery you should always start at the end and go backwards. The crowds are always at the beginning. (Alan Borg)

Aspirations

When people come to talk to you of their aspirations, count the spoons before they leave. (Logan Pearsall Smith)

Atkins Diet

Try the Atkins diet. It will probably give you a heart attack but at least you'll die thin. (Bob Geldof)

ATM Machines

Always conduct your business at ATM machines in Spanish. Your account balance will look better in pesos. (Terry Joyce)

Attacks

If you're ever attacked in the street, don't shout 'Help!' Shout 'Fire!' instead. People adore fires and always come running but everyone ignores a Help call. (Jean Trumpington)

Attractiveness

The best way for a woman to attract a man is to be naked and have a bar by the bed. (John Waters)

To attract men I use a perfume called 'New Car Interior.' (Rita Rudner)

Audiences

Always make audiences suffer as much as possible. (Alfred Hitchcock)

Autobiographies

I don't think anyone should write his autobiography until after he's dead. (Sam Goldwyn)

B

Babies

Why not have your first baby at sixty when your husband is already dead and your career is over? Then you can really devote yourself to it. (Fran Lebowitz)

Don't put 'Baby on Board' signs on your car. They're much more comfortable on cushions. (Ken Dodd)

Don't batter babies. Fry them in bread crumbs instead. (Benny Hill)

Bachelors

Never trust a husband too far or a bachelor too near. (Helen Rowland)

Don't look for a husband. Look for a bachelor. (Erma Bombeck)

I was dating a murderer. My mother advised me to stay with him. 'He's a serial killer,' I said. 'I know,' she said, 'but a *single* serial killer.' (Joan Rivers)

Down with marriage – be a bachelor like your father was! (Spike Milligan)

Backbiting

The only way to prevent people talking about you when you leave the room is never to leave the room. Don't go to lunch. Don't go to the bathroom. Wear a catheter if necessary. (Ellen DeGeneres)

If you can't say anything nice about anyone, come sit by me. (Alice Roosevelt Longworth)

Baldness

Don't waste your money on expensive cures for baldness. Just grow a big beard and stand on your head. It will have the same result. (Robert Morley)

Balls

Always bring a ball with you when you're having a game of soccer. (Ian St. John)

Bananas

A stockbroker advised me to buy a stock that would triple its value every year. I told him, 'At my age I don't even buy green bananas.' (Claude Pepper)

Bankers

When a banker jumps out a window, jump after him. That's where the money is. (Bob Monkhouse)

Banks

Nobody who robs banks should wear beige. (Mickey Rose)

If you want to steal money, don't rob a bank. Open one. (Bertolt Brecht)

Barbers

Never ask a barber if you need a haircut. He'll always say yes even if you're bald. (Dan Greenberg)

Bargaining

Don't bargain with Christ – he's a Jew. (Jimmy Swaggart)

Barmen

Never tell your troubles to the barman. It might upset his analyst. (Mort Sahl)

Baskets

Don't put all your eggs in one basket. Use an incubator. (Alan Pryor)

Put all your eggs in one basket – but watch the basket. (Mark Twain)

Bastards

Don't put all your eggs in one bastard. (Dorothy Parker)

If you're going to behave like a bastard you better be a genius. Otherwise people might not forgive you. (Jill Craigie)

Love your enemies, just in case your friends turn out to be a bunch of bastards. (R.A. Dickson)

Bathrooms

Keep your tubes of haemorrhoid ointment and Deep Heat well separated in your bathroom cabinet. (Billy Connolly)

When giving children's parties, never serve eight jugs of orangeade in a house which has only one bathroom. (Denis Norden)

The secret of a happy marriage is separate bathrooms. (Catherine Zeta-Jones)

Baths

You should take a bath once a year whether you need it or not. (Brendan Behan)

There's an advantage to not having baths. After a certain amount of time even the lice will leave you alone. (Quentin Crisp)

Baths are too hot if you have to get out immediately with agonized whooping noises and then spend half an hour reading your magazine on the bath mat. (Guy Browning)

Bath Singing

A favourite place for people who don't normally sing is in the bath because no one can throw things at you in there. The shower head also makes a perfect microphone. And everyone sounds like Pavarotti. (Guy Browning)

Batteries

Save money on batteries by taking them out of your doorbell. Then go out to the door every few minutes to see if there's anyone there. (*Viz*)

Beatings

Never beat your child with your belt – especially if you're still wearing it. (Colin Day)

Beauty

Always marry a pretty woman. That way, when you get fed up of her, you won't have any problem dumping her on someone else. (Jackie Mason)

Beef

Eat British beef. You won't get better. (Dusty Young)

Beggars

If a beggar in the street asks you for money, ask him if he has change of a tenner. When he reaches into his pocket he's rumbled. Now you don't have to give him anything. (Peter McCormack)

Beginnings

A good start is half the work. But if you don't start at all you won't even have to do half. (Jasper Carrott)

Behaviour

Never eat at a place called Mom's. Never play cards with a man called Doc. And never lay down with a woman who's got more problems than you. (Nelson Algren)

If something pleasant happens to you, don't forget to tell your friends to make them feel bad. (Casimir Montrond)

Never put anything on paper. And never trust a man with a small moustache. (P.G. Wodehouse)

Never work for a man shorter than yourself and never break wind while making love. These are the only immutable laws of life. (Richard Girling)

Beliefs

Don't believe anything until it's been officially denied. (Claud Cockburn)

My dad advised me to marry a girl with the same beliefs as my family. But I thought: Why should I marry a girl who thinks I'm a schmuck? (Adam Sandler)

Bells

Ask not for whom the bell tolls. Let the answering machine get it. (Jean Kerr)

The Bible

The Bible says you should be stoned if you sleep with a woman. I agree. (George Best)

Bigamy

Remember – the penalty for bigamy is two mothers-in-law. (Don Rickles)

Birth

A woman should never give birth after 35. 35 kids is enough for anyone. (Gracie Allen)

Don't tell your kids you had an easy birth or they won't respect you. For years I used to wake my daughter up and say, 'Melissa, you ripped me to shreds. Now go back to sleep.' (Joan Rivers)

I think the husband should always be in the delivery room, along with the child's father. (Maureen Murphy)

Somewhere on earth every ten seconds a woman gives birth. We must find this woman and stop her at once. (Sam Levinson)

Birth Control

The best form of birth control is to leave the lights on. (Lily Tomlin)

The most effective birth control I know is a toddler with nappy rash. (Kate Zannoni)

Your best form of birth control is your personality. (Chubby Brown to a heckler)

Birthdays

The best way to remember your wife's birthday is to forget it once. (Desi Arnaz)

Give your wife something with lots of diamonds on her birthday – a pack of cards. (Tommy Cooper)

I was asked how we should celebrate Harold Pinter's 50th birthday. I suggested a minute's silence. (Alan Bennett)

The best advice I was ever given was on my 21st birthday when my father said, 'Son, here's a million dollars. Don't lose it.' (Larry Niven)

There comes a time in your life when you should stop expecting people to make a big deal about your birthday. That time is age eleven. (Dave Barry)

Biscuits

Never offer a blind person a Matzo biscuit. They might think it's a page of Braille and start reading it. (Victor Lewis-Smith)

Bisexuality

Everyone should be bisexual. It doubles your chances of a date on Saturday night. (Woody Allen)

Blacks

Black people should get a fair crack of the whip. (Margaret Thatcher)

Blame

Don't blame Gordon Brown for England's problems. He did nothing. (Richard Littlejohn)

Never put the blame where it belongs. Put it where it's easiest to disregard. (Josh Fielding)

Blind People

A good trick with the blind is to stand beside them when they're about to cross the street and make that funny sound the machine makes that tells you it's safe to cross – when it isn't. (Ronald Fleming)

Bombs

Always carry a bomb with you on plane journeys. The statistical chances of another one being on board are staggeringly low. (Harriet Mills)

If you're making a bomb always use dynamite. Gelignite isn't safe. (Brendan Behan)

Bondage

Bring back the birch – but only between consenting adults. (Gore Vidal)

If you tie your girlfriend to the bed, it's important that you don't go down to the pub and get drunk afterwards. You might forget where she is. (Joseph O'Connor)

Bookmarks

Why pay a dollar for a bookmark? Use the dollar as one. (Fred Stoller)

Books

This book should not be tossed aside lightly. It should be flung with great force. (Dorothy Parker)

Never judge a book by its lover. (Kenneth Tynan)

If you don't read only one book this year, make it this one. (Malcolm Bradbury)

Boredom

If you're looking for a cure for boredom, write PTO on two sides of a piece of paper. (Hal Roach)

When you're bored with yourself, marry and be bored with someone else. (David Pryce-Jones)

Warning signs that your lover is bored: 1. Passionless kisses. 2, Frequent sighing. 3, Moved, left no forwarding address. (Matt Groening)

Galapagos turtles live as long as they do because they're so utterly boring God can't be bothered to keep a check on them. So here's how to cheat death. Be boring. Devote your life to the career of Anne Diamond. (Pamela Anderson)

Borrowing

Always live within your means even if you have to borrow to do so. (Josh Billings)

Borrow from pessimists. They never expect it back. (Red Skelton)

Bottles

If you can't open a childproof bottle, use a pliers. Or ask a child. (Bruce Lansky)

Boxing

If you're in a boxing match try not to let the other guy's glove touch your lips. You don't know where that glove has been. (Jack Handey)

There's only one thing you need to know about boxing. Never bet on the white guy. (Lennox Lewis)

Boyfriends

If you want to scare your boyfriend next Halloween, come dressed as what he fears most: Commitment. (Peter Nelson)

Save a boyfriend for a rainy day and another one in case it doesn't. (Mae West)

When you want your boyfriend to play with you, wear a full length black nightgown with buttons all over it. It's very uncomfortable but it makes you look just like his remote control. (Diana Jordan)

The best thing to do when your boyfriend walks out? Shut the door. (Angela Martin)

Bras

Feminists should be put behind bras. (Bernard Manning)

Brains

When you marry, Sally, grab a chump. Tap his forehead first. If it rings solid, don't hesitate. All unhappy marriages come from the husbands having brains. (P.G. Wodehouse)

Bread

Man shall not live by bread alone but too much butter causes cholesterol. (Ralph Gleeson)

Breakages

If it ain't broken, break it. (Johnny Rotten)

Breakfast

If you want to be sure of getting breakfast in bed, sleep in the kitchen. (Ken Dodd)

Breasts

Don't bother with women's breasts. You can't do anything interesting with them after twenty minutes. (Burt Reynolds)

Breathalyser Machines

Bars are now installing breathalyser machines that tell people if they've had too much to drink. If you've had too much, the machine warns you not to drive. And if you're really drunk, not to call your girlfriend. (Conan O'Brien)

Bribery

Never go to bed with a man until he gives you a pure white stone of at least ten carats. (Paulette Goddard)

Bridegrooms

If the bridegroom doesn't show up at your wedding, marry the best man instead. After a few weeks you won't notice the difference. (Helen Rowland)

Bridges

Don't cross your bridges till you burn them. (Dick Bower)

Don't burn your bridges while you're changing horses in midstream. (Sam Goldwyn)

Brontausari

If you live next door to a brontausarus, always bid him good morning. (Tony Hancock)

Bullies

If the school bully challenges you to a fight after class, tell him you can't wait, that you want to kick his butt right now. (Cameron Diaz)

Bungi-jumping

If at first you don't succeed, give up bungi-jumping. (Sal Heuston)

Burkhas

We should have more celebrities in burkhas. You wouldn't have to work out. We could design non-religious ones with floral prints. (Kate Beckinsale)

Buses

Don't look out for buses. It stops them coming. The driver is waiting around the corner and he simply won't budge until you stop looking for him. The only way to guarantee the bus coming is to be at the exact point where you know that running for it is absolutely futile unless you're Linford Christie. (Guy Browning)

Bushels

By all means hide your light under a bushel but be careful to point out the exact bushel under which it's hidden. (Saki)

Business Calls

When you make a business call and your secretary says, 'Will he know what it's about?' always tell her, 'Not unless he's clairvoyant.' (Carmen Rutlen)

Business Deals

When you're skinning your customers you should leave enough skin behind so you can skin them again the next time you do business. (Nikita Khruschev)

C

Cakes

They say you can't have your cake and eat it. You can, but you'll get fat. (Julian Barnes)

Camels

It may be harder for a rich man to get into heaven than it is for a camel to pass through the eye of a needle but if you have enough dosh you can buy bigger and better needles. (George Best)

Camouflage

Don't hide your bushel under a carpet. (Mel B)

Cancer

If you're going to die it's important you die of the right thing. No one wants to die from cancer. Anything else will do. (David Slattery)

Candles

It's not economical going to bed early to save on candles if the result be twins. (Chinese proverb)

Capital Punishment

We should keep the death penalty. It would result in more people being alive. (Nancy Reagan)

If you're sentenced to death you're entitled to a slap-up meal before they fry you. Go easy on the carbohydrates, though. They're bad for your cholesterol. (Russell Moore)

Hang a thief while he's young and he'll not steal when he's old. (Lord Broxfield)

Cards

When someone lays their cards on the table, count them. (Will Rogers)

Always play fairly if you have the winning cards. (Oscar Wilde)

Carrots

Eat carrots to improve your eyesight. Nobody ever saw a rabbit wearing glasses. (Steve McQueen)

Cars

Never lend your car to anyone to whom you have given birth. (Erma Bombeck)

The best way to stop the noise in the car is to let her drive. (Milton Berle)

The best car safety device is a rear-view mirror with a cop in it. (Dudley Moore)

Always treat a car like a woman. You have to coax it sometimes to get the best out of it. And at times, maybe on a difficult circuit, you have to give it a really good thrashing because that's the only way it understands. (Jackie Stewart)

Car Sales

There are some sharp practices in car sales. One of the worst is 'Cut and shut,' where two halves of cars are welded together. Look out for subtle signs of this, such as the front half of the car being a Ford Escort and the back a Vauxhall Viva. (Guy Browning)

Casinos

The best way to leave a casino with a small fortune is to go in with a big one. (Dudley Moore)

I just got back from Vegas and I have a suggestion for all the casinos. When a cocktail waitress reaches the age of sixty, let her wear pants. (Chris Mancini)

Casseroles

Avoid cooking casseroles while in revolving doors. (Bette Midler)

Catholics

My mother told me Catholics were born to suffer so I married an attorney. (Maura Lake)

Cats

Only put the cat out when it's on fire. (Les Dawson)

Don't let the cat out of the bag when the barn door is closed. (Honey Flexer)

Cemeteries

If you think you've seen everything in Paris, visit the Pere Lachasis cemetery. It boasts such immortals as Moliere, Jean de la Fontaine and Chopin. (Newspaper ad)

The best cemetery to visit in Dublin is the one in Kilbarrack. It's very healthy because it's near the sea. (Brendan Behan)

Censorship

Silence those who oppose free speech. (Peter Cook)

Chairs

Never sit on a hard chair after drinking port. (H.J. Bidder)

Change

You gotta keep changing. Shirts, old ladies, whatever. (Neil Young)

Charades

At your next party, play a version of Charades where everyone is allowed to speak what they're thinking instead of miming it. This frees up a lot of time for infinitely more interesting party games like Pin The Tail On The Donkey. (David Avedon)

Cheerfulness

If you're feeling well, enjoy it while it lasts. Because tomorrow will be much, much worse. (Philander Johnson)

If you want to cheer someone up, don't say, 'The birds are singing.' Say, 'Life is shit.' (Alain de Botton)

Chickens

Don't count your chickens before they cross the road. (Steven Wright)

Child-bearing

Do your children a favour. Don't have any. (Albert Einstein)

Never have children, only grandchildren. (Gore Vidal)

My sister was in labour for 36 hours. She got wheeled out of delivery, looked at me and said, 'Adopt.' (Caroline Rhea)

Childhood

Since childhood is a time when you prepare to be a grown-up, I think it makes a lot of sense to completely traumatise your children. Get 'em ready for the real world. (George Carlin)

Children

Children should be seen and not smelt. (Joyce Jillson)

The secret of dealing successfully with a child is not to be its parent. (Meli Lazarus)

The best way to keep your children at home is to create a pleasant atmosphere. And let the air out of their tyres. (Dorothy Parker)

There's no point discussing sex with your children. They rarely have anything new to tell you. (Bob Hope)

Chocolate

Don't wreck a sublime chocolate experience by feeling guilty. Chocolate isn't like pre-marital sex. It will not make you pregnant. (Lara Brody)

Be careful with chocolate. It can make your clothes shrink. (Ruby Wax)

Choices

If you have a choice between two things and can't decide between them, take both. (Gregory Corso)

If you're given a choice between money and sex appeal, take the money. As you get older it will *become* your sex appeal. (Katharine Hepburn)

Christians

The Jews and Arabs should sit down and settle their differences like good Christians. (Warren Austin)

Christmas

Santa Claus has the right idea: Visit people once a year. (Victor Borge)

Christmas Presents

The first rule in buying Christmas presents is to select something shiny. Even the most suspicious person will often mistake shininess for expensiveness. (P.G. Wodehouse)

Cigarettes

Don't throw cigarette butts on the floor. The cockroaches are getting cancer. (Notice in pub toilet)

If you ever read that cigarettes are bad for you, give up reading. (Denis Leary)

I don't believe in giving up cigarettes. I'm not a quitter. (Dave Allen)

Don't buy cigarettes with warning messages on the pack about lung cancer. Shop around. Mine say, 'Smoking may cause foetal injury or premature birth.' Found my brand at last. (Bill Hicks)

Clairvoyance

Don't become a clairvoyant. There's no future in it. (Jackie Mason)

Clarity

Always endeavour to eschew obfuscation. (Denis Saunders)

Cleaning Ladies

Never hire a cleaning lady called Dusty. (David Corrado)

Cliches

Avoid clichés like the plague. (Sam Goldwyn)

Clothes

Don't judge models by their clothes. There isn't enough evidence. (Bob Hope)

I was dating a transvestite. My mother said, 'Marry him. He'll double your wardrobe.' (Joan Rivers)

Always dress to match the colour of the food. (Willie Rushton)

Women should observe one basic rule in clothing. Never wear anything that panics the cat. (P.J. O'Rourke)

Dress code is everything in England. You can be a card-carrying Nazi or eat gnocci out of your navel and you won't be pilloried but don't ever, ever wear linen with tweed. (Kathy Lette)

Dress for women. Undress for men. (Angie Dickinson)

Clubs

Don't ever belong to a club that would have you as a member. (Groucho Marx)

Coalmines

Have a dirty weekend. Explore an old coalmine. (Mark Kavanagh)

Cocaine

Stay away from cocaine. It may seem glamorous at the beginning but one day, one day it will be your turn to buy. (Emo Philips)

Cockroaches

Never eat in a restaurant where you see a cockroach bench-pressing a burrito. (Pat McCormick)

The only way to get rid of cockroaches is to tell them you want a long-term relationship. (Jasmine Birtles)

Coffee

Don't drink English coffee. It isn't much more than toasted milk. (Christopher Fry)

Never drink coffee at lunch. It will keep you awake in the afternoon. (Jilly Cooper)

Coffins

Try our coffins and you'll never want to use any other ones. (notice on undertaker's window)

Colonic Irrigation

If you want to clear your system out, sit on a piece of cheese and swallow a mouse. (Johnny Carson)

Comedy

The secret to all comedy writing is: Write Jewish and cast Gentile. (Robert Kaufman)

Coming Out

It's not a good time to tell your father you're gay when you're in a moving vehicle. (Kate Clinton)

If you tell people you're gay when you're on a plane you get the whole row to yourself. Say, 'I swear to God, sir, I'm a lesbian. If you don't move, I'll touch your wife up during the movie.' (Suzanne Westenhoefer)

People sometimes ask me if they should tell their mother they're gay. I say, 'Never tell your mother anything!' (Quentin Crisp)

Committees

To get something done, a committee should consist of no more than three men, two of whom are absent. (Robert Copeland)

Commitment

Ladies, do not expect us guys to make hasty commitments. And by 'Hasty' I mean, 'Within your lifetime.' (Dave Barry)

Competitiveness

Don't try to keep up with the Joneses. It's much cheaper to drag them down to your level. (Quentin Crisp)

Don't meet competition. Crush it. (Charles Revson)

Completion

You should always finish everything you st   (Nigel Rees)

Computer Dating

All computers should assemble at their local factory for dating tips. (Kevin Stewart)

Computer Programming

Beware of computer programmers who carry screwdrivers. (Leonard Brandwein)

There are basically two ways to programme computers. But only the third one works. (Bill Gates)

The best way to re-boot a computer is with your foot. (John Cleese)

Condoms

Buy me and stop one. (Message on machine dispensing condoms)

At the chemist shop, a good idea is to blow a condom up as big as it will go and then say to the assistant, 'I'm just checking to see if it will fit.' (Adrian Edmondson)

Irish people tend to wear two condoms. To be sure, to be sure. (Alice Baldwin)

Condoms aren't completely safe. A friend of mine was wearing one last week and he got hit by a bus. (Bob Rubin)

Confucius

Confucius him say that if man want to grow a row of corn, first he must shovel a ton of shit. (Stephen King)

Confucius him say too fucking much. (Ernie Kovacs)

Constipation

Use Moses' cure for constipation. Take two tablets and go up a mountain. (Larry McCabe)

Colds

Never fight colds. That's what makes a cold sore. (Leopold Fechtner)

Cooking

Don't taste the food while you're cooking it. It may make you lose the resolve to serve it. (Phyllis Diller)

Contentment

If you're foolish enough to be contented, don't show it. Grumble with the rest. (Jerome K. Jerome)

Contraceptives

Contraceptives should be used on every conceivable occasion. (Spike Milligan)

Contact Lenses

Everyone should wear contact lenses whether they need them or not. (Morrissey)

Conversation

Talk to a man about himself and he'll listen for hours. (Benjamin Disraeli)

If you're ever at a loss to support a flagging conversation, introduce the subject of eating. (Leigh Hunt)

Beware of the conversationalist who adds 'In other words.' He is merely starting afresh. (Christopher Morley)

Coroners

If you want to become a coroner, be prepared for a stiff examination. (John Crosbie)

Corporal Punishment

Let's re-introduce corporal punishment in schools – and use it on the teachers. (P.J. O'Rourke)

Courting

Better be first with an ugly woman than hundredth with a pretty one. (Pearl S. Buck)

It's bad manners to begin courting a widow before she's home from the funeral. (Seamus McManus)

Curtains

The first pull of the cord always sends the curtains in the wrong direction. So start with the second one. (Andrew Boyle)

Cremation

Cremation is cheaper than burial. Undertakers are now charging the earth. (Des MacHale)

Save energy. Get cremated with a friend. (Kenny Everett)

Cricket

Cricket shouldn't be used as a political football. (David Graveney)

Crime

Crime may not pay but the hours are good. (Woody Allen)

If the crime rate went down by 100% it would still be fifty times higher than it should be. (John Bowman)

To make sure crime doesn't pay, the government should take it over. (Norman Collis)

Critics

Pay no attention to the critics. Don't even ignore them. (Sam Goldwyn)

Crying

Beware of men who cry. They may be in touch with feelings but it's usually only their own ones. (Nora Ephron)

Men only cry when assembling furniture. (Rita Rudner)

Never cry over a man. Just yell, 'Next!' (Denise Gilbert)

Curiosity

If at first you don't succeed, pry, pry again. (Philip Hanson)

Curtseying

Curtsey while you're thinking what to say. It buys you time. (Lewis Carroll)

Customs

When sneaking through Customs with something to declare, always approach the oldest official. No chance of promotion. (W. Somerset Maugham)

CVs

Never enclose a photograph of yourself on a CV for a job application unless specifically requested to do so. People won't like it unless you look absolutely gorgeous. And if you look absolutely gorgeous, they'll assume you're thick. (Guy Browning)

Cycling

Cycling is a good thing for youngsters. It keeps them off the streets. (David Bean)

D

Dalmations

Dalmations shouldn't be dressed in polkadot or indeed any type of monochrome. Unless they specifically request it. (Jo Wheaton)

Danger

Beware of the first few moments of life because they're very dangerous. The last few can be pretty dodgy too. (Jim Gardner)

Dating

The best kind of girl to date is one who owns a pub above a racecourse and turns into a pizza after sex. (Duncan Barber)

If your man says, 'Your place or mine?' at the end of the date you should reply, 'You go to your place and I'll go to mine.' (Bette Midler)

My father always said, 'Be the kind they marry, not the kind they date.' As a result I used to nag guys for dishwashers on first dates. (Kris McGaha)

I've been advised to date older men. That just about leaves God. (Joan Rivers)

Daydreaming

Don't daydream on office time. You might miss the coffee break. (Jilly Cooper)

Death

Don't die if you can help it. It's bad for your health. (Zero Mostel)

Die now, pay later. (Sign on undertaker's window)

The best way to die is to sit under a tree, eat lots of bologna and salami, drink a case of beer and then blow up. (Art Donovan)

Debts

Pay your debts with a smile, though cash is often preferred. (Brian Bruce)

Never get deeply in debt to anyone who cried at the end of *Scarface*. (Robert Wieder)

Defeat

When you're 4-nil up you should never lose 7-1. (Lawrie McMenemie)

Delegation

If you want something done, ask a busy man. He'll have his secretary do it. (Phyllis Gates)

Dentists

Never go to a dentist who has blood in his hair. (William Ruskin)

Don't go to dentists who've had their surgeries soundproofed. (Milton Berle)

Desertion

If you leave a woman you probably ought to shoot her. (Ernest Hemingway)

Despair

Don't despair, not even over the fact that you don't despair. (Franz Kafka)

Dessert

Seize the moment. Remember all those women who waved aside the dessert tray on the Titanic. (Erma Bombeck)

Diamonds

I never hated a man enough to give him his diamonds back. (Zsa Zsa Gabor)

Never trust a man who doesn't have an instant hormonal response to diamonds. (Kate Reardon)

Diaries

Never travel without a diary. One should always have something sensational to read on a journey. (Oscar Wilde)

Never be without a diary. They're full of indispensable information, like the recommended tyre pressure for North Korea. (Leslie Mallory)

Keep a diary and one day it'll keep you. (Mae West)

Dieting

The best reducing exercise is to shake your head violently from side to side when offered a second helping. (Kay Finch)

My diet tips are: Don't eat breakfast, don't eat lunch and don't eat dinner. (Karl Follett)

The best diet I ever heard of was the one that told you you could eat anything you wanted. The only problem was, you had to do it naked in front of a mirror. (Rodney Dangerfield)

Eat, drink and be merry for tomorrow ye diet. (William Gilmour)

The only thing you lose on the average diet is your sense of humour. (Oprah Winfrey)

It's time to go on a diet when you're standing next to your car and you get a ticket for double parking. (Totie Fields)

Dinner

Don't ask a child what he wants for dinner unless he's buying. (Fran Lebowitz)

At a dinner party one should eat wisely but not too well and talk well but not too wisely. (W. Somerset Maugham)

Directions

When you come to a fork in the road, take it. (Yogi Berra)

Never ask an English person for directions. They're too polite to tell you if they don't know the way and will send you somewhere else instead – probably Wales. (Joseph O'Connor)

Diseases

Never transmit a sexual disease in public. (Robert Mills)

Distractions

Occasionally the woman in your life will become possessive and insecure. She will say things like, 'You don't love me,' even though you saw her twice last year. Rest assured, these moments will pass. Just do something to distract her as she's going through her crisis, like putting out the bins. (Richard Ziegler)

Divas

Never go across the alley even to dump garbage unless you're dressed to the teeth. (Cecil B. de Mille to Paulette Goddard)

Diving

Don't dive into water on an empty stomach. Always go in head first. (Leopold Fechtner)

Divorce

Never marry a man you wouldn't want to be divorced from. (Nora Ephron)

My mother always said, 'Don't marry for money. Divorce for money.' (Wendy Liebman)

I highly recommend divorce at all costs. Well maybe not at all costs. Anything under $4 million. (Tom Arnold)

A divorce can only be called successful if the party you throw to celebrate it has more guests than the wedding. (Chloe Sevigny)

Divorce takes too long. Just live with a woman you don't like for a while and then give her your house. (Rod Stewart)

DIY

When all else fails, read the instructions. (Agnes Allen)

Doctors

My doctor told me to avoid excitement so I've started watching Milwall. (Les Dawson)

Don't have any tests when you go to the doctor. There's always a danger he'll find something wrong with you. (David Slattery)

My doctor told me to watch my drinking. Now I do it in front of the mirror. (Rodney Dangerfield)

My doctor told me to stop drinking or it would endanger my health. He's dead now. (George Best)

Never go to a doctor whose office plants have died. (Erma Bombeck)

Doctors' Appointments

Avoid waiting for a doctor's appointment by making one for nine o'clock every morning. If you wake up feeling well, simply phone up and cancel it. (*Viz*)

Documents

Destroy all my old documents - but keep copies. (Sam Goldwyn to his secretary)

Dogs

Don't make the mistake of treating your dogs like humans or they'll treat you like dogs. (Martha Scott)

Dog Owners: Don't waste money on a lead. Simply walk your dog backwards holding its tail. (*Viz*)

If you're a dog and your owner suggests you wear a sweater, suggest he wear a tail. (Fran Lebowitz)

Donald Trump

Ten things Donald Trump should do to assure people he's a fit president:

1.

2.

3.

4.

5.

6.

7.

8.

9.

10.

Doubt

When in doubt, mumble. (Chic Murray)

When in doubt, file under 'Haven't got a clue.' (Simon Henchard)

Dresses

Beware of the man who picks your dresses. He probably wants to wear them. (Erica Jong)

Always wear long dresses. They cover a multitude of shins. (Mae West)

Drinking

Don't drink on an empty stomach. Have a few beers first. (Ken Dodd)

Don't drink on an empty head. (Frank Skinner)

You'll never find the answer to your problems at the bottom of a glass. Drink from the bottle instead. (Ronnie Scott)

Don't buy a drink for the road. The road is already laid out. (Flip Wilson)

Don't drink. It makes you feel too good. (Oscar Levant)

Never ask an Irish person how many drinks he's going to have on a given night. He wouldn't understand the question. (Tommy Tiernan)

Far better than sex is the pleasure of drinking at someone else's expense. (Sil Fox)

Drink Driving

If you drink, don't drive. Don't even putt. (Dean Martin)

If your wife has driven you to drink, make her walk to the pub. (Hal Roach)

Don't drive to the pub. You can never remember where you parked the car after you come out. (Dave Allen)

Don't drink and drive. It spills when you turn the corner. (Tony Hancock)

Drink Mixing

Never allow your children to mix drinks. It's unseemly. And they use too much vermouth. (Fran Lebowitz)

Driving

When driving, always make sure you have a car. (Leopold Fechtner)

The most important thing a mother has to learn about driving is how to do it with your child's hands over your face. (Katherine Whitehorn)

The problem with the designated driver programme is that it's not a desirable job. If you ever get suckered into it, have some fun for yourself. At the end of the night drop everyone off at the wrong house. (Jeff Foxworthy)

When you're driving behind people on cell phones it's generally wise to wait patiently for a few moments until they ram into a bridge abutment. Then you can pass safely on whatever side has the least amount of flame spewing out. (Dave Barry)

The cardinal rule for driving in Ireland is: When in doubt, accelerate. (David Monaghan)

Drugs

Always say no to drugs. It will drive the prices down. (Gene Krasna)

Don't do drugs because you'll end up in prison. And drugs are very expensive in prison. (John Hardwick)

Avoid all drugs. The only dope worth shooting is Donald Trump. (Michael Moore)

Advice to kids: Get high on sports, not drugs. But if there are no sports in your neighbourhood, get high on drugs. (George Carlin)

The best way to smuggle drugs these days is to stuff them up a dog's arse. The airport officials will think the sniffer dogs are just getting frisky. (Ardal O'Hanlon)

Cannibalise legalis. (Graffiti)

Drunkenness

Be always drunk. Nothing else matters. (Charles Baudelaire)

Always do sober what you said you'd do drunk. That will teach you to keep your mouth shut. (Ernest Hemingway)

Sheets can be kept clean by getting drunk and falling asleep in your clothes. (Big O)

A man ought to get drunk at least twice a year on principle so he won't allow himself to get snotty about it. (Raymond Chandler)

Anyone who can't get drunk by midnight ain't trying. (Toots Shur)

Drycleaning

Don't spend £2 to dryclean a shirt. Donate it to the Salvation Army instead. They'll clean it for you and put it on a hanger. Then you can buy it back for 50p. (Jack Dee)

Dumping

When I want to end a relationship I just say, 'I want to marry you so we can live together.' Sometimes they leave skid marks. (Rita Rudner)

Agony aunts tell us we should tell the man in our life how to make love to us. That wouldn't work with me. When I told my last boyfriend how to knot his tie he dumped me. (Alanis Penforth)

If you want to dump your girlfriend, there are some good things you can do. For instance, play charades and mime 'Fuck off.' Or ask her if she was once a man. Or say things like, 'Guess what I just found up my nose.' (Adrian Edmondson)

Dummies

If you ever fall off the Sears Tower, go real limp. You'll look like a dummy and people will try to catch you. Because, hey, free dummy. (Jack Handey)

Duty

An author's first duty is to let his country down. (Brendan Behan)

Early Rising

Always get up early if you're hitch-hiking. You'll avoid the traffic. (Des MacHale)

Early to bed and early to rise, makes you feel stupid and have really red eyes. (Shirley Brooks)

Early to rise and early to bed, makes a man healthy, wealthy and dead. (James Thurber)

Earthquakes

Here's a good thing to do during an earthquake. Straddle a big crack in the ground. If it opens wider, go 'Whoa! Whoa!' and flail your arms around like you're going to fall in. (Jack Handey)

Eating

Never eat on an empty stomach. (Dawn French)

Never eat anything at a sitting that you can't lift. (Miss Piggy)

Eat here and you'll never eat anywhere else again. (Notice on restaurant window)

Economising

Never economise on luxuries. (Angela Thirkell)

Save a little money each month. By the end of the year you'll be surprised at how little you have. (Ernest Haskins)

Ecstacy

Don't take Ecstacy if you're visiting a Holocaust museum. (Sean Hughes)

Effectiveness

If you think you're too small to be effective you've never been in bed with a mosquito. (Betty Reese)

Effort

Why be difficult when, with a little extra effort, you can be impossible? (Percy Grainger)

There are no useless efforts. Sisyphus was developing his muscles. (Roger Callois)

Electric Toothbrushes

The older models of electric toothbrushes tend to have the same engines as pneumatic drills so you have to brace yourself against the bathroom walls to stop yourself being shaken bodily into the shower cubicle. (Guy Browning)

Elephants

If an elephant appears in your living-room, put the crockery out of sight before you offer him a cup of tea. (Noel Coward)

When you have an elephant by the hind legs and he's trying to run away from you, it's probably best to let him. (Abraham Lincoln)

If you're an elephant on the edge of a cliff hanging onto a daisy by your trunk, don't sneeze. (Hank Rafter)

Elevators

It's not a good idea to use elevators during fires. Fire extinguishers are better. (Bernard Manning)

Empathy

Before you criticise someone, walk a mile in their shoes. That way you're a mile away from them after your criticism. And you have their shoes. (Frieda Norris)

Enemas

Don't use enemas. They're useless. From my experience you might as well shove them up your arse. (Frankie Howard)

Enemies

Keep your friends close but your enemies closer. (Mario Puzo)

Do not fear when your enemies criticise you. Beware when they applaud. (Charles Bukowski)

If you're bored with the enemies you have and want to make new ones, tell two of your women friends they look alike. (Mignon McLaughlin)

English

English is the perfect language to sell pigs in. (Michael Hartnett)

Epidurals

Epidurals shouldn't just be given for the birth. They should be given for the conception as well. (Cher)

Ethics

Grub first, then ethics. (Bertolt Brecht)

Eurovision Song Contest

There's one thing you need to do if you're commenting on the Eurovision Song Contest. Always have a whiskey before song seven. (Terry Wogan)

Evening Classes

The most important thing to remember when signing on for an evening class is to have absolutely no interest in the subject. That will free you up to devoting all your attention to the main purpose of the class, i.e. meeting your Significant Other. After you've divorced you'll have lots of time to brush up on the bits you missed. (Sue Alcock)

Exam Cheating

A good way to cheat at exams is to write trigonometrical formulae on your arms and then fabricate a diarrhoea attack to get into the loo to read them. If you have a nervous temperament, though, this might bring on an actual diarrhoea attack. And it's difficult to read trigonometrical formulae while evacuating your bowels. (Bert Brohler)

Excess

You can't have everything. Where would you put it? (Steven Wright)

I wouldn't recommend sex, drugs or insanity for everyone but they always worked for me. (Hunter S. Thompson)

Too much of a good thing can be wonderful. (Mae West)

Excretion

Sex isn't as important as excretion. A man can go 70 years without a piece of ass but he can die in a week without a bowel movement. (Charles Bukowski)

Exercise

The two best exercises in the world are dancing and making love. A simpler one is standing on tiptoe. (Barbara Cartland)

What do I do to stay fit? Pass the vodka bottle. (Keith Richards)

Exercise is bunk. If you're healthy you don't need it. If you're sick you shouldn't take it. (Henry Ford)

My doctor told me to get more exercise and fresh air. I said I'd drive with the window open. (Angus Walker)

Exclamation Marks

Cut out all the exclamation marks in your writing. They make it look as if you're laughing at your own joke. (F. Scott Fitzgerald)

Expectation

Don't look forward to the day you stop suffering. When it comes, you'll know for sure you're dead. (Tennessee Williams)

Experimentation

One should try everything once in life except incest and folk dancing. (Arnold Bax)

Eyes

Keep your eyes wide open before marriage and half shut afterwards. (Benjamin Franklin)

Remember to look both ways before crossing your eyes. (Roger McGough)

Throwing acid is wrong - in some people's eyes. (Jimmy Carr)

F

Faces

After forty a woman has to choose between losing her face or her figure. My advice is: Keep your face and stay sitting down. (Barbara Cartland)

Facts

A good storyteller never lets the facts get in the way. (Dave Allen)

Get your facts first. Then you can distort them as much as you please. (Mark Twain)

If facts conflict with the legend, print the legend. (John Ford)

You must never face facts. I've never faced facts in my life. If I had, I would have realised that I was a plain little girl from Quincy, Massachusetts and never gone on the stage. (Ruth Gordon)

Failure

They say we learn more from failure than success. That's why it's important to keep failing. You'll become a total fuck-up in the process but at least you'll be an educated one. (Keith Broe)

Go on failing. Only next time, try to fail better. (Samuel Beckett)

Family Planning

Every family should have at least three children. Then if one of them is a genius, the other two can support him. (George Coote)

I believe in large families. Every woman should have at least three husbands. (Zsa Zsa Gabor)

I've always told my friends they should have one husband and seven children. But I ended up with seven husbands and one child. (Lana Turner)

Family Trees

There's bugger all point tracing your family tree. If Darwin got it right, your great-great-great-great grandfather was an amoeba. And if the Old Testament is right, you stem from someone who ate his brother and pulled his mum. (Jeremy Clarkson)

Fancy Dress Balls

May I suggest, sir, that if you want an impenetrable disguise for the fancy dress ball that you go sober? (Samuel Foote to a drunk acquaintance)

Fans

Make your fan last longer. Hold it still and shake your head from side to side. (Clive Dempsey)

Fantasies

If you fantasise about being president of the U.S., move to the White house for a few days to indulge it. If the real president asks you what you're doing there, shuffle a few papers on the desk to make yourself look important. This always works. (Jo Keynes)

Farewells

When taking leave of one another we often say, 'Be well.' Good wishes should be more realistic. We should amend that to, 'I hope you remain reasonably healthy during the next 18 months or so. If you have a stroke I hope it only paralyses you on one side, leaving you free to take phone calls.' (George Carlin)

Farting

There's no easy way to acquire the skill of farting. Success can only be achieved through practice and beer. Women may be able to produce more delicate flatulence with champagne. (P.J. O'Rourke)

Never let off without letting on, especially in an elevator. (Kevin Burns)

Fashion

Don't despise fashion. It's what we have instead of God. (Malcolm Bradbury)

Never let a panty line show around your ankle. (Joan Rivers)

Fat Farms

Visit a Fat Farm and eat all around you. Argue that if it was meant to induce slimming it would have been called a Thin Farm. (Jackie Gleason)

Fatherhood

The time not to become a father is eighteen years before a war. (E.B. White)

There's one absolute rule about being a successful father. When you have a kid, don't look at it for the first two years. (Ernest Hemingway)

Faults

Before criticising your wife's faults, pause to consider the fact that if it wasn't for them she might have told you to take a flying fuck for yourself. (Kenny Everett)

Feet

Don't put both feet in your mouth at the same time. If you do you won't have a leg to stand on. (Fred Allen)

Feminism

I don't go with feminism. My advice is, find a rich guy with a heart problem and marry him. Then creep up behind him and say, 'Boo!' (Joan Rivers)

Fiancés

It's always a good idea to have a meal with your intended before you get married. If he doesn't gross you out while he's eating there's a slim chance you might be able to spend the rest of your life with him. (Liz Hurley)

Fighting

If anything is worth fighting for, it's worth fighting dirty for. (Lynn Connolly)

Get your retaliation in first. (Marlon Brando)

He who fights and runs away lives to avoid the next tussle as well. (Edith Keyes)

Filing

Always mess up your files. This makes sure the secretary can be blamed if you've lost something. (Jill Simpson)

Films

The best way to make a successful film is to make the subtleties obvious. (Billy Wilder)

If you're going to make a rubbish film, make sure you're the best rubbish in it. (Richard Burton)

The length of a film should be directly related to the endurance of the bladder. (Alfred Hitchcock)

Don't improve it into a flop. (Sam Goldwyn)

If Robert Redford gets interested in your script, delete any scenes where he might be laughing. (Joe Eszterhas)

Film Plots

If your film has no plot, cut the intermission. That way the audience won't get a chance to discuss it until it's over. (Paddy Chayevsky)

Fingers

After shaking hands with a Greek, count your fingers. (Aristotle Onassis)

When your daughter's date picks her up, sprinkle some dust on her before she goes out. Tell him it makes fingerprinting easier. (Mike McQueen)

Finland

I think we should have Finland removed as a country. We don't need it. (George Carlin)

Fires

My father used to say, 'Always fight fire with fire.' Which is probably why he got thrown out of the Fire Brigade. (Harry Hill)

If your home burns down on you, rescue the dogs. At least they'll be faithful to you. (Lee Marvin)

Avoid chip pan fires by suspending a plastic bag full of water over the pan when you cook. If a fire occurs, the bag will melt and the water will extinguish the flames. (*Viz*)

Fish

Give a man a fish and you feed him for a day. Give him a fishing rod and you can shag his wife all day long. (Sean Killeen)

Flattery

Flattery is all right as long as you don't inhale. (Adlai Stevenson)

There's a saying that flattery will get you everywhere. Be careful, though, because you could tell someone how nice their hair looks and end up in Swindon. (Guy Browning)

Flattery will get you nowhere but don't stop trying. (Lois Maxwell)

If you're flattering a woman, it pays to be subtle. You don't have to do this with men because they believe any compliment automatically. (Alan Ayckbourn)

Flirting

There are times not to flirt. When you're sick, for instance, or when you're with children. Or when you're on the witness stand. (Joyce Jillson)

Try to bed every woman you meet. You get slapped a lot but you get fucked a lot too. (Warren Beatty)

Flossing

Never floss a stranger. (Janeane Garofalo)

Flowers

Don't leave flowers by the side of the road. They cause accidents. (Milton Jones)

Say it with flowers. Hit him over the head with a bouquet. (Roseanne)

Flying

Don't fly on any airline where the pilot believes in reincarnation. (Henny Youngman)

If you're about to fly around the world on a hot air balloon, don't forget the toilet paper. (Richard Branson)

Followers

If a million people follow you, ask yourself where you went wrong. (Indira Gandhi)

Food

Don't feed the hand that bites you. (Theodora Fitzgibbon)

Never let your caloric intake exceed your white blood cell count. (Beth Donahue)

Fools

There's no fool like an old fool. Ask a young fool if you don't believe me. (Ken Dodd)

Suffer fools gladly. They may be right. (Holbrook Jackson)

Football

The secret of football is to equalise before the other side scores. (Danny Blanchflower)

There are two ways of getting the ball in football. One way is from your own players. That's the only way. (Terry Venables)

Playing with wingers is more effective against European sides like Brazil than English ones like Wales. (Ron Greenwood)

The best thing for this team to do is to stay at nil-all until they score a goal. (Martin O'Neill)

The first ninety minutes of a game are the most important. (Bobby Robson)

Forecasts

Never make forecasts, especially about the future. (Sam Goldwyn)

Forgiveness

Forgive your enemies. It will drive them nuts. (Eleanor Doan)

One should forgive one's enemies, but not before they're hanged. (Heinrich Heine)

The stupid neither forgive nor forget. The naïve forgive and forget. The wise forgive but do not forget. (Thomas Szasz)

Turn the other cheek too often and you'll get a razor through it. (Johnny Rotten)

Fortune Tellers

Advice on God, love and parking. (Notice on fortune teller's window)

Fouling

Don't foul like a wimp. If you're gonna foul, knock the crap out of him. (Norm Stewart)

Foxholes

Never share a foxhole with anyone braver than you are. (H.L. Mencken)

Free Will

We have to believe in free will. We have no choice. (Isaac Bashevis Singer)

Friends

To find a friend one must close an eye. To keep him – two. (Norman Douglas)

Fruit

Don't squeeze the fruit. Ask for Debbie. (Sign in shop)

People who live in chateaux/Should never throw tomateaux. (J. B. Morton)

Fudge

Avoid any diet that discourages the use of fudge. (Roseanne)

Always serve too much hot fudge on hot fudge sundaes. It makes people overjoyed, and forever in your debt. (Judith Olney)

Fuel

Fuel is more effectively delivered *a la cart* than *coal-de-sack.* (Noel Purcell)

Funerals

Funerals in Ireland should be called funferalls. (James Joyce)

Always go to other people's funerals or they won't go to yours. (Yogi Berra)

There's nothing like a morning funeral to sharpen the appetite for lunch. (Arthur Marshall)

Funerals are depressing. Don't even go to your own one. (Brian Behan)

Fur

If you want to keep your dog in line, walk him past the fur shop a couple of times a week. (George Carlin)

Never buy fur from a veterinarian. (Bette Midler)

Don't buy fur. For every coat you get, twenty trees have to be cut down to make the protest postcards. (Emo Philips)

G

Gambling

The race isn't always to the swift nor the battle to the strong but that's the way to bet. (Damon Runyon)

Never go for a 50/50 shot unless you're 80/20 sure. (Ian Darke)

Statistically speaking you have just as good a chance of winning the lottery if you don't buy a ticket. (Bob Monkhouse)

Garden Centres

Avoid garden centres. There's nothing more depressing than being dragged round one on a Sunday morning – especially if you don't have a garden. (Jeff Green)

Geese

Geese should be skein and not herd. (Colin S. Jarman)

Generalisations

Never generalise. (Sid Caesar)

German

Life is too short to learn German. (Richard Porson)

Gifts

What do you give a man who has everything? Antibiotics! (Robin Williams)

My attitude to sex is simple. Get it over quickly and then get a gift. (Joan Rivers)

Gin

Never drink anything stronger than gin before breakfast. (W.C. Fields)

To drink gin properly you have to be female, 45, and sitting on the stairs. (Dylan Moran)

Giraffes

If you're a giraffe, a sore throat is a surefire excuse for getting off work. (Mark Greenway)

Avoid reading pop-up books about giraffes. (Sean Lock)

Glasses

Never hit a man with glasses. Use a brick instead. (Jo Brand)

Glasshouses

They say people in glasshouses shouldn't throw stones. They should, but not at the glass. (John Gielgud)

People who live in glasshouses should breathe on the windows. (Michael Hordern)

Gloves

Buy waterproof gloves. Then you can wash your hands without getting them wet. (Lynn Frederick)

Don't touch shit, even with your gloves on. The gloves get shittier but the shit doesn't get glovier. (Ferenc Molner)

God

People who use God as a weapon should have their limbs amputated. (Bob Dylan)

Let's all give God a big hand. I've seen the last page of the Bible and everything works out all right. (W.C. Fields)

Why attack God? He may be as miserable as we are. (Erik Satie)

Trust in God. She will provide. (Emmeline Pankhurst)

God is love but get it in writing. (Gypsy Rose Lee)

Gorillas

In a tussle with a gorilla we should relax the Queensbury Rules. (Ernest Hemingway)

Golf

Never try to keep more than 300 separate thoughts in your head during your golf swing. (Henry Beard)

The secret of winning the U.S. Open is: Shoot a lower score than anyone else. (Ben Hogan)

The secret of missing a tree in golf is to aim straight at it. (Michael Green)

My advice to struggling golfers is to take two weeks off. Then quit the game. (Jimmy Demaret)

Don't talk to golf balls. It won't do you any good unless you do it while your opponent is teeing off. (Bruce Lansky)

'Play it as it lies' is one of the fundamental dictates of golf. The other is, 'Wear it if it clashes.' (Henry Beard)

My wife gave me the answer to my putting problems. She said, 'you need to hit the ball closer to the hole.' (Ben Hogan)

There's one important rule they need to introduce in golf. You should be able to strike your opponent if he's in the lead. (David Feherty)

Grammar

Don't. Ruin. The. Flow. Of. Your. Writing. (Doris Lessing)

Remember to never split an infinitive. The passive voice should never be used. Do not put statements in the negative form. Proof-read carefully to see if you words out. And don't start a sentence with a conjugation. (William Safire)

They also serve who punctuate. (Mark Twain)

Grass

If the other fellow's grass looks greener, let him worry about cutting it. (Paddy Murray)

Greetings

Don't tell your friends about your indigestion. 'How are you?' is a greeting, not a question. (Arthur Guiterman)

Always pat children on the head whenever you meet them, just in case they happen to be yours. (Augustus John)

G Spots

There are three things beginning with G that we should avoid: golf, gardening and gonorrhoea. (Dom Joly)

Guests

If you're having people over for a meal, serve steaming hot coffee early on. If a guest burns his tongue he won't be able to taste anything afterwards. (Phyllis Diller)

The first rule of visitor hospitality is that the guest must never get a glimpse of the conditions in which you normally live. (John D. Sheridan)

Guns

The right to bear arms for civilians makes about as much sense as the right to arm bears. (Lenny Bruce)

You can get farther with a kind word and a gun than you can with a kind word. (Al Capone)

Never fire a gun at your body unless you're trying to injure yourself. (Mel Brooks)

The Centre for Disease Control reports that guns are now the second biggest cause of premature death in America, just behind AIDS. So if you have unprotected sex, don't use a gun. (Johnny Robish)

Gyms

Have you been to the gym lately? Boy, some of those guys over-
develop. If your neck is as wide as your head, take a day off.
(Margaret Smith)

The best way for a guy to impress a girl in a gym is with pull-ups. Pull
up in a Corvette. Pull up in a rolls Royce. Pull up in a
Cadillac...(Conan O'Brien)

Gynaecology

Gynaecologists – after a hard day at the orifice, look up a friend.
(Bruce Ridley)

H

Hair

Never trust a man who combs his hair from the left armpit. (Alice Roosevelt Longworth)

Hamlet

You can't make a Hamlet without breaking egos. (Peter O'Toole)

Hammers

Keep hitting yourself with a hammer. It's lovely when you stop. (Terry Cooper)

Hands

Don't bite the hand that lays the golden egg. (Sam Goldwyn)

Hand Signals

Always use hand signals when you're driving your car. The index finger and forefinger usually get the best results. (Brendan O'Connor)

Hannibal Lecter

Hannibal – why not have a friend over for dinner? (Graffiti)

Happiness

It's pretty hard to tell what brings happiness considering both poverty and wealth have failed. (Kin Hubbard)

Money doesn't make you happy. I have $50 million now but I was just as happy when I only had $49 million. (Arnold Schwarzenegger)

I told my daughter to get married, have a child, get divorced and live happily ever after. (Cher)

Hats

A hat should be taken off when you greet a lady. And then left off for the rest of your life. (P.J. O'Rourke)

The best way to fight a woman is with your hat. Grab it and run. (John Barrymore)

Always wear a hat so you'll know where to stop washing your face. (Eric Idle)

Heads

Never marry a man with a big head. You're going to give birth to his child. You want a baby with a narrow head. (Jilly Golden)

Headaches

I always found I got a headache when I drank coffee. Then one day my wife found the solution. 'Take out the spoon,' she suggested. (Bob Monkhouse)

Nothing acts faster than Anadin. So if you have a headache, take nothing. (Bunny Carr)

Health

Always take care of your health. Then you won't die of anything serious. (Tony Butler)

The best drink you can take for your health is Irish coffee. It contains the four main life-saving ingredients: alcohol, coffee, sugar and fat. (Alex Levine)

Become a Christian Scientist. It's the cheapest health plan out there. (Betsy Salkind)

Health is the thing you need most of all when you're sick. (Tony Butler)

I know a man who gave up smoking, drinking and rich food. He was healthy right up to the day he shot himself. (Johnny Carson)

Heart Attacks

It's okay to have sex after a heart attack. Just make sure you close the ambulance door. (Phyllis Diller)

Hearts

Don't waste your time trying to break a man's heart. Be satisfied if you can manage to just chip it in a brand new place. (Helen Rowland)

Don't wear your heart on your sleeve. It's very uncomfortable that way. (John Cleese)

Heart Transplants

If you're a singer, having a heart transplant in America might be a good idea. You'll be able to sing 'I Left My Heart in San Francisco' with more conviction. (Michael Green)

Heat

If you can't stand the heat, get out of the oven. (Forrest Gump)

If you can't stand the heat in the dressing-room, get out of the kitchen. (Terry Venables)

If you can't stand the heat, stay in the kitchen but move closer to the fridge. (Bill Cosby)

Heaven

Just in case heaven is like the IRS, make sure you get a receipt every time you do a good deed. (Bob Hope)

Heaven for the climate, hell for the company. (J.M. Barrie)

Heayy Breathers

If a heavy breather comes on the phone, simulate an asthma attack to get back at him. Then tell him to call again. (Lily Tomlin)

Hen Parties

Liven up your hen party. Tattoo the name of the best man onto the Bride-o-gram. (Pamela Stephenson)

The hen night should be held sufficiently in advance of the wedding to allow for complete recovery following a liver transplant. (Jenny Éclair)

Hesitation

She who hesitates is won. (Oscar Wilde)

He who hesitates is bossed. (Henny Youngman)

If you think before you speak, the other fellow gets his joke in first. (Ed Howe)

Holidays

Next year for the holidays my wife said she wants to go somewhere she's never been. I said, 'Try the kitchen.' (Les Dawson)

Take your holidays in winter. The deck chairs are cheaper. (Kenneth Williams)

Hollywood

Strip away the phony tinsel of Hollywood and you'll find the real tinsel underneath. (Oscar Levant)

If you want to be a success in Hollywood, go to New York. (Bert Lahr)

Hollywood is no place for a woman to find a husband – especially her own. (Denise Dercel)

The only way to avoid Hollywood is to live there. (Igor Stravinsky)

There's a group in Hollywood called Divorce Anonymous. It works like this. If a member of the group starts to feel the urge to divorce, they send over an accountant to talk him out of it. (Sean Connery)

Homosexuality

There's nothing wrong with going to bed with someone of the same sex. We should draw the line at goats. (Elton John)

Gay's okay but hetero was bettero. (Michael Delaney)

I think we should have gays in the army. At least then *someone* would admire the uniforms. (Elayne Boosler)

Homosexuals should be castrated with rusty nails. (Brendan McGahon)

God save the queens! (Kenny Everett)

Homelessness

It's not so bad for the homeless in winter. They should buy a plane ticket and go somewhere hot like the Caribbean where they can eat free fish all day. (Lady Victoria Hervey)

Honesty

Honesty may be the best policy but it's important to remember that dishonesty is the second best one. (Cyril Connolly)

Mother always said honesty was the best policy and that money wasn't everything. She was wrong about a lot of other things too. (Gerald Barzan)

Honeymoons

The best way to save money on the honeymoon is to go alone. (Les Dawson)

Hooliganism

I've been asked what I would do about hooliganism in football. I said, 'Let's start with the 92 club chairmen.' (Brian Clough)

Horns

Cars should have silent horns so they wouldn't wake people up at night. (Bill Shipton)

If you're driving in the Third World, only honk your horn under the following conditions 1. When anything blocks the road. 2. When anything doesn't. 3. When anything might. 4. At red lights. 5. At green lights. 6. At all other times. (P.J. O'Rourke)

Horoscopes

Never trust horoscopes. Typical Piscean mistake. (Russell Harty)

Horses

Don't walk around the rear end of a horse. Their timing is perfect. (Lester Piggott)

Horses' Heads

If you feel like killing someone, don't do it. It's against the law and you'll feel terrible afterwards. To get the anger out of your system do something more casual instead, like, say, putting a horse's head in their bed like they do in the *Godfather* films. But don't kill the horse. It wouldn't be nice – especially for the horse. Just wait until you see one lying around somewhere. Country areas are best. (Mitch Goldberg)

Horticulture

You can bring a whore to culture but you can't make her think. (Dorothy Parker)

Hosts

If you want to be the perfect host, try to make your guests feel at home when you wish they were. (W.A. Nance)

Houses

People who live in stone houses shouldn't throw glass. (Austin O'Malley)

Housekeeping

Housework, if it's done right, can kill you. (John Skow)

Housework can't kill you but I figure why take the chance. (Phyllis Diller)

Be a good housekeeper. Every time your husbands divorce you, keep the house. (Zsa Zsa Gabor)

Hucklebuck

If you're attacked by a lion in the jungle, confuse it by dancing the hucklebuck. Lions generally aren't familiar with this dance and it will confuse them – especially if you know all the right moves. (Steve Lawrence)

Hull

All those of you contemplating visiting Hull, please adjust your calendars to 1957. (Philip Larkin)

Husbands

A husband should be older, heavier, uglier, taller and hoarser than his wife. (Edgar Howe)

Every wife should be entitled to a middle husband she can forget. (Adele Rogers St. John)

Trust your husband. Love your husband. But get as much as you can in your own name. (Joan Rivers)

There's so little difference between husbands, you may as well keep the first one. (Adele Rogers St. John)

Hygiene

Wash your hands and say your prayers because Jesus and germs are everywhere. (Kinky Friedman)

Always wash your hands thoroughly. You never know where the soap's been. (Sidney James)

Hypochondria

The best cure for hypochondria is to forget about your body and get interested in someone else's. (Goodman Ace)

Hypotheses

It is a good morning exercise for a research scientist to discard a pet hypothesis every day before breakfast. (Konrad Lobenz)

Ice

Don't put ice in my drink. It takes up too much room. (Groucho Marx)

All ice cubes should be boiled before using. (U.S. army notice during typhoid epidemic)

Idleness

Don't stand around doing nothing. People will think you're a workman. (Brendan Grace)

Better to have loafed and loved than never to have loafed at all. (James Thurber)

Immortality

I don't like the idea of dying. It's been done before. (George Burns)

Don't try to live forever. You will not succeed. (George Bernard Shaw)

Impetuosity

Think twice before saying nothing. (Eldridge Smyth)

Impulses

Distrust your first impulses, especially if they're good ones. (Tim Carlton)

Impotence

To succeed with the opposite sex, tell her you're impotent. She won't be able to wait to disprove it. (Cary Grant)

Incest

It's very bad form to screw your children – except in your will. (P.J. O'Rourke)

Indecision

If you don't know what to do, walk fast and look worried. (Scott Adams)

Independence

Encourage independence in your children by regularly losing them in the supermarket. (Rosaleen Linehan)

Indifference

Don't let your indifference bother you. (Buddy Hackett)

Individuality

Always remember that you're absolutely unique. Just like everyone else. (Margaret Mead)

Indulgence

An absolutely sacred rite of life is the smoking of cigars and the drinking of alcohol before, after, and, if need be, during meals. And in the intervals between them. (Winston Churchill)

Infanticide

Infanticide is a terrible crime and should not be practised at any time, particularly if a child is teething. (Donald Greenberg)

Inferiority Complexes

Try to make your inferiority complex better than everyone else's one. (Norma Shore)

Infidelity

Never be unfaithful to a lover, except with your wife. (Al Kobenz)

Philanderers: Avoid the embarrassment of shouting out the wrong name in bed by only having flings with girls who have the same name as your wife. (*Viz*)

Never tell your wife you've cheated. Even if she walks in on you, deny it. Say, 'Honey, this chick came in with a sign around her neck saying, "Lay on top of me or I'll die."' She'll buy it every time. (Lenny Bruce)

Thou shalt not commit adultery – unless you're in the mood. (W.C. Fields)

Influence

The best time to influence the character of a child is about 100 years before he's born. (William Ralph Inge)

Initials

Never trust a writer who uses his initials. (A.A. Gill)

Innovation

Don't be afraid to try new things. Remember, a lone amateur built the ark and a large group of professionals built the Titanic. (Greg Knight)

Insanity

If you ever go temporarily insane, don't shoot somebody like a lot of people do. Just try and get some weeding done. (Jack Handey)

Insomnia

A recent study conducted by the American Medical Association shows that sleep loss may be linked to weight gain. So the next time someone asks you if you've put on a few pounds, say, 'My husband snores.' (Caroline Rhea)

The best cure for insomnia is to get a lot of sleep. (Sean Hughes)

Insults

Never call women bitches. Choose a more gender-neutral term like 'Asshole.' (Daniel Liebert)

My father told me never to insult anyone unintentionally. So if I insult you, you can be goddam sure I mean it. (John Wayne)

If you insult someone, try to water it down so you don't offend them too much. In other words, if you say to a person who's been annoying you, 'You're the lowest form of protoplasm that ever crawled out of the fucking earth,' do so with a smile on your face. That takes all the harm out of it. (Doug Peterson)

Integrity

This above all to thine own self be true and it must follow as the night the day, you'll die a pauper. (Sandra Knowles)

To thine own self be false. Who else will know? (Denis Goodwin)

Intimidation

Let the man in your life know who's boss from the start. If he makes a pass at you, pull down his trousers and say, 'Not until that gets a bit bigger.' (Wendy Hiller)

If anyone intimidates you, imagine them sitting in long red underwear on the lavvie. (Ronnie Barker)

Insurance Policies

Be careful with insurance. The downside of having a massive policy on your life is that you can never have another bath without the nagging fear that your spouse is about to drop a toaster into it. (Guy Browning)

Investment

Never put money in anything that eats or needs re-painting. (Billy Rose)

Invitations

Only invite people to your house when you know you won't be there. They won't turn up anyway so no damage is done. (Gore Vidal)

IQ Tests

At the age of 16, everyone should take a simple IQ test. If they can't name four cabinet ministers, three American rivers and two characters from *Cannery Row*, it's vasectomy time. (Jeremy Clarkson)

Irony

Strike while the irony is hot. (Don Quinn)

Irish Dancing

Only one part of the body must not move during an Irish dance – the bowels. (Jack MacHale)

Irish dancing requires a stiff upper hip. (John Crosbie)

Italians

Never let a dago by. (Simon Cassidy)

J

Jackets

Keep your jacket tightly buttoned if you want to hide the shirt you don't have on. (Owen Kelly)

Jeans

Don't look for your sexuality in your genes. Look for it in your jeans. (Jo Henderson)

Never wear fly-button jeans when you're on a bender. (Spike Milligan)

Jobs

Always suspect any job men willingly vacate for women. (Jill Tweedie)

A sure way to keep a job is to get things so mixed up on your first day that the boss can't afford to fire you. (Bill Bowyang)

If you can't get a job as a pianist in a brothel, become a royal reporter. (Max Hastings)

Jobs are very competitive these days. If you're not fired with enthusiasm you'll be fired with enthusiasm. (Leopold Fechtner)

If you want to lose your job, wave your nob out the window while shouting the company's name. Or send bum prints to dispatch for distribution around the office, marked 'Urgent.' (Adrian Edmondson)

Job Interviews

When you go for a job interview, a good thing to ask is if they ever press charges. (Jack Handey)

At job interviews always tell them you're willing to give 110%. Unless the job is that of a statistician. (Adam Gropman)

Jogging

My doctor told me jogging could add years to my life. I said, 'Yeah, since I took it up I feel ten years older.' (Lee Trevino)

Jog and die healthier. (Fred Allen)

Jokes

Don't make jokes at the European Parliament. The Germans only get them ten minutes after the Swedes. (Glenys Kinnock)

When all else fails, go for the dick joke. (Robin Williams)

Journalism

If you don't get the big story then you have to trash it. It's the law of the Fleet Street jungle. (Piers Morgan)

Jungles

Life is a jungle. Become king of the jungle. Turn yourself into a lion. (Tony Hancock)

Juries

If you want to get out of jury duty, turn up with neat hair and tidy clothes. That means a guilty verdict. (Mary Kenny)

K

Kayaks

You can't have your kayak and heat it too. (Sean Gilmartin)

Kicking

Never kick a man when he's up. (Tip O'Neill)

Kindness

Kill people with kindness. They'll die happy. (Kenneth Williams)

Kinkiness

Date married men. They don't want anything kinky – like breakfast. (Jani Rodgers)

Never ask for a *menage-a-trois* on a first date. (Kim Henley)

Be creative – invent a perversion. (Lenny Bruce)

Kissing

Kissin' don't last, cookin' do. (George Meredith)

It is not considered proper to frenchkiss your grandmother goodnight – especially if she's not staying over. (John Freeman)

It takes a lot of experience to kiss like a beginner. (*Ladies Home Journal*)

Never let a fool kiss you or a kiss fool you. (Joey Adams)

Never let a guy kiss you on a first date – if you can get him to do more. (Joan Rivers)

Kitchens

Guys – don't argue with a woman in the kitchen. We know where everything is and you don't. (Diane Amos)

Knees

The best way to drive is with your knees. It frees your hands up for putting on lipstick and talking on the phone. (Sharon Stone)

Don't touch a woman's knee if you're sitting at a meal with her. A woman has an instinctive knack of knowing if you're doing this to caress her or merely to wipe your greasy fingers on her stocking. (George Moore)

Lapdancing

If you're going to a lapdancing club, sport your most ludicrous watch and your most ridiculous cufflinks. Let's face it. If you look like a millionaire the girls are far more likely to drag their nipples over your face. (Dylan Jones)

Laughter

We must laugh before we are happy for fear of dying before we have laughed at all. (Jean de la Bruyere)

Don't give me any of that 'Laughter is the best medicine' stuff. If I get strep throat I'd much rather take penicillin than watch any Benny Hill re-runs. (Ellen DeGeneres)

Make a married woman laugh and you're half way there. (Michael Caine in *Alfie*)

The key to lasting love isn't how beautiful your partner is but whether she makes you laugh. So look out for opportunities to see your loved one falling off buses, tripping down the stairs of busy restaurants or getting herself tangled up in barbed wire fences. (Jeff Green)

The Law

If you like laws and sausages you should never watch either of them being made. (Otto von Bismarck)

If you want justice, go to a whorehouse. If you want to get fucked, go to court. (Richard Gere)

Laxatives

If you can't afford laxatives just sit on the toilet with a Stephen King book. (Ken Dodd)

Laziness

Hard work pays off in the end. But laziness pays off now. (Al Lubel)

Leaders

To lead the people, walk behind them. (Lao-Tzu)

Don't follow leaders. Watch your parking meters. (Bob Dylan)

Leapfrog

Never play leapfrog with a unicorn. (Louis Safian)

Learning

We should live and learn. But by the time we've learned, it's too late to live. (Carolyn Wells)

Never learn to do anything. If you can't do it you'll always find someone else to do it for you. (Mark Twain)

When teaching your baby to talk, point to an object and say, 'Where is the nearest public library in Serbo-Croatia, please?' Baby will then think that's what it's called. (Adrian Edmondson)

Legs

The players are tired. Bobby Robson should be thinking of throwing some fresh legs on. (Kevin Keegan)

Never trust men with short legs. Their brains are too near their bottoms. (John Gielgud)

Leisure

People would have more leisure time if it wasn't for all the leisure time activities that use it up. (Peg Bracken)

Swimming is a good hobby to take up, especially after a relationship ends. It's great exercise, and when you get to France you can have croissants. (Cathy Hopkins)

Lesbians

Catholic girls make the best lesbians. All their life they're told, 'Don't have sex with men. It's a sin.' And they're like, 'I'm okay with that.' (Judy Carter)

Lessons

If you must give your child lessons, send him to a driving school. He's far more likely to end up owning a Datsun than a Stradivarius. (Fran Lebowitz)

Letters

Never take any notice of anonymous letters unless you get a few thousand of them on the same subject. (Robert Menzies)

When you get to 60, re-read all the letters you've kept over the years. Thankfully you don't have to answer them now. (Thora Hird)

Letter from problem page: 'I'm in love with a beautiful girl but she doesn't even know I'm alive.' Reply: 'Show her your birth certificate.' (Jane Powers)

Don't worry about begging letters if you win the lottery. You can keep sending them. (Foggy Spellman)

Lettuce

Don't eat lettuce in Mexico unless it's been sterilised by a blowtorch. (Benjamin Kean)

Liars

If you want to be thought a liar, always tell the truth. (Logan Pearsall Smith)

Never tell a lie except for practice. (Mark Twain)

If one cannot invent a really convincing lie it is often better to stick to the truth. (Angela Thirkell)

Libraries

The first thing to have in a library is a shelf. From time to time this can be decorated with literature - but the shelf is the main thing. (Finlay Peter Dunne)

Life

Life is too short to stuff a mushroom. (Shirley Conran)

Knock hard. Life is dead. (Arnold Wesker)

Lifts

Don't accept lifts from strange men – and all men are strange.
(Robin Morgan)

Light

Many hands make light work. In the event of a power failure, get all
your friends to put them in the air and it will come back. (Michael
Sheridan)

There's nothing wrong with making love with the light on. Just make
sure the car door is closed. (George Burns)

Limitations

Life is about accepting your limitations. If you want to become a
concert pianist and you've never played the piano in your life, this is
unrealistic. Become a rocket scientist instead. (Tony Penny)

Lips

The best way to keep a stiff upper lip is to starch your moustache.
(Tony Blackburn)

Liposuction

If you're serious about losing weight, liposuction works every time. At least if you regain consciousness. (David Slattery)

Lipstick

The important thing with lipstick isn't the colour but to accept God's final decision about where your lips end. (Jerry Seinfeld)

Liquor

Candy is dandy but liquor is quicker. (Ogden Nash)

How should a French woman hold her liquor? By the ears. (Peter Sammons)

Litter

I know how we could cure the litter problem in a day. Give every blind person a pointed stick. (Ken Dodd)

Loans

Don't lend people money. It gives them amnesia. (Gene Perret)

Never lend money to a man who runs his office from a phone booth. (Rita Rudner)

London

Help clean London up. Eat a tourist. (Paul Cash)

Loneliness

If you're afraid of loneliness don't get married. (Anton Chekhov)

Longevity

Get revenge on your children. Outlive them. (George Cohen)

Iron gates last forever. Afterwards you can make horseshoes from them. (Sir Boyle Roche)

The secret to a long and happy life is the saliva of young girls. (Tony Curtis)

The secret to a long life is to keep breathing. (Sophie Tucker)

The secret to a long life is: Swim, dance a little, go to Paris every August...and live within walking distance of two hospitals. (Horatio Luro)

Looking Younger

If you want to look younger, rent smaller children. (Phyllis Diller)

The best way to look younger is not to be born so soon. (Charles Schulz)

If you want to look young and thin, hang around with old fat people. (Jim Eason)

If she looks old, she's old. If she looks young, she's young. If she looks back, follow her. (Bob Hope)

Los Angeles

Don't run out of milk if you live in L.A. There are no shops over there. (Deirdre O'Kane)

Loss

The easiest way to find something you've lost is to buy another one. The original will turn up the following day. (Leonard Rossiter)

When you've lost something and start looking for it, you always find it in the last place you look. So look in the last place first. (Billy Connolly)

Love

Better to have loved and lost than never to have lost at all. (Samuel Butler)

Better to have loved and lost than to have paid for it and not enjoyed it. (Sid Caesar)

Better to have loved and lost than to have married her, had a shitload of children and been forced to attend all those boring PTA meetings. (Joseph Glynn)

Luck

I'm not a believer in luck but I do believe you need it. (Alan Ball)

Depend on a rabbit's foot for luck if you will but remember it didn't work for the rabbit. (R.E. Shay)

Lunch

Whenever you want to marry someone, have lunch with his ex-wife. (Shelley Winters)

M

Magic

Break the ice at dinner parties with a stunning set of tricks. Beware of losing your concentration, though, if you're doing a 'Sawing a woman in half' one. A man I know did this and it almost proved fatal. Luckily, the woman is now living contentedly in Scarborough. And Devon. (Cathy Hopkins)

Malice

Never attribute to malice that which can be adequately explained by stupidity. (Aldous Huxley)

Manure

Always keep a pile of manure on the kitchen table. It keeps the flies off the food. (John Dineen)

Marathons

If you want to know what you'll look like in ten years time, look at yourself in the mirror after you've run a marathon. (Jeff Schaff)

Marriage

By all means marry. If you get a good wife you'll be happy. If you get a bad one you'll become a philosopher. (Socrates)

The ideal marriage would be between a deaf husband and a blind wife. (Padraic Colum)

They ought to re-write the words of the marriage ceremony to read, 'In sickness and in hell.' (Bette Davis)

My parents' marriage left me with two convictions. One, that human beings should not live together. And two, that if they have any children, they should be taken away from them at an early stage in life. (Philip Larkin)

Don't marry on an empty stomach - or a starved libido. (John Travolta)

The old theory was: Marry an older man because they're more mature. The new theory is: Men don't mature. Marry a younger one. (Rita Rudner)

Marry in haste, repent in Reno. (Hedda Hopper)

Always marry in the morning. That way, if it doesn't work out you haven't wasted the whole day. (Mickey Rooney)

Martini

When pouring martini, make sure it's filled dangerously close to the brim. (Joe McGuirk)

Mascara

Don't wear mascara if you're in love with a married man. (Shirley MacLaine)

Meditation

Take up meditation. It beats sitting around all day doing nothing. (Paul Rudd)

Memory

The best way to remember something is to tie a string around your finger. The best way to remember to tie a string around your finger is to tie a second one around another finger, or maybe a toe or some other part of your anatomy. You'll need a good bit of string for all this. I can't think of any way of helping you to remember to buy the string. (Jane Asquith)

Men

If you catch a man, throw him back. (Andrea Dworkin)

I've started to go out with older men. When my friends ask me, 'Is he cute?' I'm like, 'At this stage I'll just settle for a healthy prostate.' (Maura Lake)

There are two times in your life when you're going to have trouble with men: 1. Before marriage. 2. After marriage. (Cher)

Menopause

Don't worry about the menopause. Worry about the men who don't. (Bette Midler)

Merriment

Eat, drink and be merry. Tomorrow you may be radioactive. (Conan O'Brien)

Eat, drink and be merry. Tomorrow they may make it illegal. (David Niven)

Milk

If this note blows away, please knock. (Notice to milkman on Cork doorstep)

The best way to keep milk from turning sour is to leave it in the cow. (Niall Toibín)

Don't cry over spilt milk. It makes it much harder to clean up. (Kay Graham)

Minds

Your mind is a dangerous neighbourhood. Don't go there at night. (Christiana Northrup)

Always speak your mind whether you mean it or not. (Rodney Dangerfield)

Mirrors

A beautiful woman should break her mirror early. (Balthasar Gracian)

If you're ever on fire, don't look in a mirror. That will really get you into a panic. (Jack Handey)

Never believe mirrors or newspapers. (John Osborne)

When we're buying clothes we go into these little cells with mirrors everywhere so we can see what's wrong with our body from every conceivable angle. After you leave these rooms they should offer you some kind of counselling, or at least have a sticker on the mirror that says, 'Caution: Objects seen here may appear larger.' (Rita Rudner)

Mistakes

You must learn from the mistakes of others. You can't possibly live long enough to make them all yourself. (Sam Levenson)

You're making progress if each mistake you make is a new one. (Hilare Belloc)

To make mistakes is human; to profit from them divine. (Kin Hubbard)

I'm glad I never paid attention to good advice. Had I abided by it I might have been saved from some of my most valuable mistakes. (Gene Fowler)

Never interrupt your enemy when he's making a mistake. (Napoleon)

If I had my life to live over I'd make the same mistakes, only sooner. (Tallulah Bankhead)

Mistresses

Buy old masters. They fetch much better prices than old mistresses. (Lord Beaverbrook)

Marry your mistress. It creates a job opportunity. (Greg Knight)

Moderation

Practise everything in moderation, including moderation. (Samuel Fuller)

Modesty

A woman who goes to bed with a man ought to lay aside her modesty with her skirt and put it on again with her petticoat. (Michel de Montaigne)

Money

Never talk about money to people who have either more or less of it than you have. (Fred Metcalf)

If you find a million dollars on the street, give it up. It could belong to a poor person. (Gene Perret)

Make your money go farther. Post it to a distant relative. (John Crosbie)

Monogamy

If you're looking for monogamy you better marry a swan. (Nora Ephron)

Most men think monogamy is a type of furniture. (Britt Ekland)

Monuments

When smashing monuments, save the pedastals. They always come in handy. (Stanislaus Lec)

Morals

Never let your sense of morals get in the way of doing what's right. (Isaac Asimov)

Mormons

A Mormon told me they don't drink coffee. I said, 'A cup of coffee every day gives you wonderful benefits.' He said, 'Like what?' I said, 'Well it keeps you from being a Mormon for one thing.' (Emo Philips)

Mothers

My mother taught me everything I needed to know in life. Don't talk to strangers. Don't pay retail. And the size of your hair should always match the size of your ass. (Stephanie Schiern)

A tip to all new mothers: Don't go to bed with your baby. You might fall asleep, roll over on it and put your back out. (Harry Hill)

Motives

Never ascribe to an opponent motives meaner than your own. (J.M. Barrie)

Mothers-in-Law

However much you dislike your mother-in-law, you must not set fire to her. (Ernest Wild)

Be kind to your mother-in-law. Babysitters are expensive. (Leopold Fechtner)

For Mother's Day do something nice for the lady. Take her out to dinner. Send her flowers. Divorce her daughter. (Joey Adams)

If you must choose between living with your mother-in-law and blowing your brains out, don't hesitate. Blow out hers. (Les Dawson)

Mount Everest

If you've decided to climb Mount Everest and you're susceptible to head colds, bring a good scarf. (Minty Crane)

Mousetraps

Build better mousetraps and you will catch better mice. (George Gobel)

Mud Wrestling

Don't mud wrestle with a supermodel in her jacuzzi – unless she asks you to. (Hugh Hefner)

Muggers

The best way to avoid being mugged when you're in the bad end of town is to walk like a mugger. Don't walk like a muggee. (Billy Connolly)

Multi-tasking

One of the best ways to multi-task is to read in the loo. (Jo Brand)

If you're drinking and smoking in a standing position, tip your ash into the can to save yourself having to look for an ashtray. Then when you're finished you can pee into it. (Joe Morley)

Murder

Never murder a man when he's committing suicide. (Woodrow Wilson)

If you decide to murder your wife, do so early on in the marriage. That way, you might have time to marry again after you get out of jail. (Bernard Manning)

If you're a sniper working from the top of a building, try to pick off people who are having a bad day. And never commit only one murder. You wouldn't serve a meal with only one course, would you? (P.J. O'Rourke)

Murder is always a mistake. One should never do anything one can't talk about at dinner. (Oscar Wilde)

Music

Don't listen to too much Wagner. It might give you the urge to conquer Poland. (Woody Allen)

Buy our Band-Aid record. You can be assured the money will literally go into someone's mouth. (Bob Geldof)

Musicians

My advice to young musicians is to break windows, smoke cigars and stay up late. (Tom Waits)

N

Nailbiting

Don't bite your nails. Look what happened to Venus de Milo. (Bob Monkhouse)

The best way to get a man to stop biting his nails is to make him wear shoes. (Greg Knight)

Names

Save money on expensive personalised number plates by simply changing your name to match your existing plates. (*Viz*)

Never allow your child to call you by your first name. He hasn't known you long enough. (Fran Lebowitz)

If you tend to forget people's names it's always better to make one up rather than just call them nothing. It also helps if the name you make up sounds like their real one. This can pose problems if you're talking to Jack and you call him Jacqueline. (Baz Miles)

When picking your children's names, make sure they end with vowels. That way, when you call them, it carries. (Bill Cosby)

Don't call your child Arthur. Every Tom, Dick and Harry is called Arthur these days. (Samuel Goldwyn)

Don't date any woman whose father calls her Princess. She usually believes it. (Don Rickles)

Nappies

Nappies are a nuisance and an unnecessary expense. Instead have your baby fitted with a septic tank that only needs emptying once a month. (Adrian Edmondson)

Having a child at 60 would be nice. You could both be in nappies at the same time. (Sue Kolinsky)

Never change nappies in midstream. (Frank Skinner)

Naples

See Naples and die – from the smog. (Joseph O'Connor)

Neighbours

Love your neighbour but make sure his wife doesn't find out. (Red Skelton)

The two worst things in life are neighbours and haemorrhoids. The difference is, you can do something about haemorrhoids. (Spike Milligan)

Nervous Breakdowns

If you're going to have a nervous breakdown, try to have it at home where nobody will know about it. It pisses people off having to visit you in the psychiatric ward. (Tony Hancock)

Newspapers

To appreciate newspapers you have to read between the lies. (Goodman Ace)

Always believe what you read in the newspapers. It makes them so much more interesting. (Rose Macaulay)

Nicotine Patches

Nicotine patches are the best way to help you give up cigarettes. Stick one over each eye and you can't find them. (Brendan O'Carroll)

Niceness

Be nice to your children. They're the ones who'll choose your nursing home. (Cyril Connolly)

Be nice to the people you meet on the way up. You'll meet them on the way down as well. (Wilson Mizner)

You don't have to be nice to people on the way up if you're not coming back down. (Colonel Tom Parker)

Nicknames

Don't call people nicknames unless their name is Nick. (Jimmy Patterson)

Non-Conformity

This year be a non-conformist like everyone else. (Wendy Hiller)

Noses

If your nose goes on strike, picket. (Dave Barry)

Never pick your nose while you're working with superglue. (Emo Philips)

Novels

There are just three rules for writing novels. Unfortunately nobody knows what they are. (W. Somerset Maugham)

Every novel should have a beginning, a muddle and an end. (Peter de Vries)

The only advice I have to give to a young novelist is to fuck a really good agent. (John Cheever)

Nudity

Many a true word is spoken undressed. (H.L. Mencken)

If you want to see nudity, don't go to a theatre. Go to a Turkish bath. (Noel Coward)

Numbers

To really annoy people, shout random numbers at them while they're counting something. (Mike McQueen)

Always look out for number one. And be careful not to step into number two. (Rodney Dangerfield)

O

Obituaries

An interesting experiment would be to die so you can read your obituaries. If possible, come back from the dead and haunt the people who wrote bad ones. (John Belushi)

Old People

Never ask old people how they are if you have anything else to do that day. (Joe Restivo)

If you have elderly people living with you, cut back on their heat and light. Old people often exaggerate how cold they feel. (George Carlin)

One Night Stands

I don't believe in that one night thing. I think people should get to know someone and even be in love with them before they use and degrade them. (Steve Martin)

Opticians

If you can't see what you want here, ring the bell. (Notice on optician's window)

Opportunities

All too often after opportunity knocks, by the time you push back the chain, unlock the bolts and shut off the burglar alarm, it's too late. (Rita Coolidge)

Never miss an opportunity to have sex or appear on television. (Gore Vidal)

Oral Contraceptives

The best oral contraceptive is the word 'No.' (Wendy Lieber)

Oral Sex

Oral sex is to be recommended. Mainly because it's the only way most of us can get our partners to shut up. (Dennis Hanley)

Women like oral sex to go on a long time. To strengthen your relationship I suggest getting your snorkel out, putting *Tubular Bells* on the hi-fi and cancelling the milk. (Jeff Green)

Never do anything to a clitoris with your teeth that you wouldn't do to an expensive waterproof wristwatch. (P.J. O'Rourke)

Some men love performing oral sex on us ladies. If you find such a man, treat him well. Feed him caviar and don't let your girlfriends catch a glimpse of him. (Cynthia Heimel)

You know the worst thing about oral sex? The view. (Maureen Lipman)

Orang-Utans

If you're doing a tango with an orang-utan on an ice rink when both of you are drunk, it's customary to let him lead. (Petra Ilich)

Oranges

If you learn to peel an orange in your pocket you won't have to share it with anyone else. (Niall Toibin)

Hollywood is a great place to live if you're an orange. (Fred Allen)

Don't become a poet. You'll find yourself crawling around a carpet in some hotel room at 3 o'clock in the morning looking for a word that rhymes with 'orange.' (Leonard Cohen)

Orphans

Men, take my advice and marry an orphan. First of all there are never any in-law problems. Second, there are no annoying Thanksgiving and Christmas visitors sitting around pretending to enjoy the company of a couple of fifth generation nitwits. And when it comes to visiting her folks, the worst thing that might happen to you would be an occasional trip to the cemetery to leave some cheap flowers. (George Carlin)

Overtaking

The best way to overtake a car on a narrow road is to stay behind it. (Tony Butler)

Overtakers keep undertakers busy. (William Ewart Pitts)

Ownership

My father always told me, 'Own the land you live on. Then you can piss on it without being arrested.' (Richard Harris)

P

Pacemakers

I asked my doctor what I should do after having my pacemaker put in. He said, 'Keep paying your electricity bill.' (Roger Moore)

Painting

Never accept an unsigned painting from a surrealist. You won't know which way to hang it. (Ian Mitchell)

If you're painting a ceiling, a good rule of thumb is that there should be at least as much paint on the ceiling as on your hair. (P.J. O'Rourke)

It doesn't matter how badly you paint as long as you don't paint badly like other people. (George Moore)

Anyone who paints a sky green or fields blue ought to be sterilised. (Adolf Hitler)

Pancakes

Put popcorn in your pancakes and they'll turn over by themselves. (Suzy Wiseman)

Panic

If you're in a situation of extreme distress, don't panic. Count to ten. If you're still distressed after counting to ten, then panic. (Richard Dix)

Paparazzi

If you're being chased by the paparazzi, don't drive fast. Just find a really expensive parking lot. That'll get rid of them in record time. They won't want to pay the charge. (James McAvoy)

Parachutes

If the ripcord on your parachute fails to open, amuse your friends by flailing your arms on the ground and pretending to swim. (Rory Byrne)

Parenting

I only have two rules for my daughter. She will dress well and she will never have sex. (John Malkovich)

When dealing with immature behaviour such as nose-picking or genital fondling, try to be discreet so your child won't make fun of you when you do it. (P.J. O'Rourke)

When a kid turns thirteen, stick him in a barrel, nail the lid shut, and feed him through the knothole. When he turns sixteen, plug the hole. (Mark Twain)

Parking

The best way to solve the parking problem is to buy a parked car. (Joe Cuddy)

Always put 'Pay and Display' tickets upside down in the centre of your windscreen in the hope that the parking warden will crick his neck trying to read them. (*Viz*)

Give a woman an inch and she'll park a car on it. (E.B. White)

Parties

Never refuse a drink at a party or people will assume you're an alcoholic. Nine times out of ten they'll be right. (Michael Greene)

Remember: a dog isn't just for Christmas, it's for life. So be careful at that office party. (Jimmy Carr)

At the Christmas office party one should never forget to photocopy one's bum and place it on the bosses' desk. (Paul Johnson)

Any date will do for a party but ugly ones are more likely to be game for a Mongolian Cluster Fuck or Portsmouth Pig Pile. (P.J. O'Rourke)

Party Games

A good party game is to stand on one leg on a table and try to rub your stomach and pat your head at the same time. You'll usually find the patting turns into the rubbing and vice versa. A few hours later you'll probably find the other partygoers gazing at you strangely. It is now time to (a) begin crying, (b) get drunk, or (c) put your head in the oven. (Chloe Gibson)

The Past

Don't pre-judge the past. (Gene Wilder)

If you go back in time, be careful not to step in anything. (Matt Groening)

The only way of preventing what is past is to put a stop to it before it happens. (Sir Boyle Roche)

Patience

You have to have a lot of patience to learn how to have patience. (Stanislaus Lec)

If my patients had patience I wouldn't have so many patients. (Dr Abraham Low)

Patriotism

Ask not what your country can do for you but what you can do for your country. (John F. Kennedy)

Ask not what you can do for your country. They're liable to tell you. (Mark Steinbeck)

Peanut Butter

If you want peanut butter in bed while you're having sex and your partner doesn't, the thing to do is to find another partner. (Dr Ruth Westheimer)

Pedestrians

A pedestrian should be legally allowed to toss at least one hand grenade at a motorist every day. (Brendan Francis)

Penguins

The two healthiest things to eat are chicken and fish. What you should do is combine them. Eat a penguin. (Dave Atell)

Periods

Better late than pregnant. (Julie Birchill)

Persistence

If at first you don't succeed, try again. Then give up. There's no point in being a damn fool about it. (W.C. Fields)

Perspective

In order to ensure that you keep a sense of perspective in life, pin a picture of a supermodel on your kitchen wall. Then write above it, 'Today someone, somewhere, is taking her shit.' (Tom Lowe)

Persuasion

If you can't convince 'em, confuse 'em. (Harry S. Truman)

Perversion

Never stick your genitals into anything you're not certain they'll come out of. (P.J. O'Rourke)

Petrol

All those in favour of saving petrol raise your right foot. (Road sign)

Save petrol the Irish way. Push your car to work. (Sil Fox)

Philanthropy

Remember the poor. It costs nothing. (Josh Billings)

Philately

Stamp out philately. (Rhod Gilbert)

Philosophy

I have a simple philosophy: Fill what's empty. Empty what's full. And scratch where it itches. (Alice Roosevelt Longworth)

Phones

I don't think phone sex is a good idea. There's always a danger of getting your finger stuck in the 9. (Michael Mee)

Photographs

Should you be a teenager blessed with uncommon good looks, document this state of affairs by the taking of photographs. It is the only way anyone will believe you in years to come. (Fran Lebowitz)

If you look like your passport photo you're too ill to travel. (Hal Roach)

Pianos

Surgeons – never try to take out a man's appendix while he's moving a grand piano. (Scott Siegel)

When a piano piece gets difficult, make faces. (Arthur Schnabel)

Pick-up Lines

You want a good pick-up line? Here it is. 'Hi, I'm Hugh Hefner.' (Hugh Hefner)

Piercings

At fifty, confine your piercings to beer cans. (Olympia Dukakis)

Pigs

Never wrestle with a pig. You both get dirty and the pig likes it. (W.C. Fields)

Pills

A pill can save you from a headache and a headache can save you from the pill. (Rosita Sweetman)

Pimps

Never ask your wife if she still hears from her old pimp. (Johnny Carson)

Planes

They should have 'Boring' and 'Non-Boring' sections in airplanes just like they have 'Smoking' and 'Non-Smoking' ones. Then you wouldn't have to fight the urge to jump off in mid-flight if someone is telling you about their gall bladder operation. (Buddy Hackett)

Don't worry about plane crashes. In the event of an accident the pilot is always first on the scene. (Max Kauffman)

They should make the whole plane out of that stuff that's in the black box. (Steven Wright)

There are two reasons to sit in the back of an airplane. Either you have diarrhoea or you're anxious to meet people who do. (Henry Kissinger)

Always travel in the rear of a plane. You never hear of them backing into mountains. (Frank Carson)

Plastic Surgery

If you live in Los Angeles it's a good idea to have breast implants. An A-cup entitles you to handicapped parking. (Jeannie Dietz)

Never go to a plastic surgeon whose favourite artist is Picasso. (Pete Burns)

Plays

The first rule for a young playwright is not to write like Henry Arthur Jones. The second and third rules are the same. (Oscar Wilde)

Let him who is without sin stone the cast first. (Howie Schneider)

Pockets

A gentleman shouldn't talk to a lady with his hands in his pockets unless she's his wife. In which case it's unavoidable. (Lennie Lower)

Poetry

If you're going to write, write one poem all your life. Let nobody read it and then burn it. (Jack Nicholson)

The reason most people don't care about poetry is because most poets don't care about people. (Tony Curtis)

Live in a barrel. Break your head with a hatchet. Plant tulips in the rain. But don't write poetry. (Charles Bukowski)

Poison

Never drink from bottles marked 'Poison.' They won't taste nice and they'll probably give you a pain in your tummy. (Rikki Fulton)

Police

Save police time. Beat yourself up. (Joe Orton)

Politicians

Make your local politician work for a change. Don't re-elect him. (Sean Kilroy)

Politicians are like nappies - they need to be changed often. And for the same reason. (Pat Shortt)

Politics

If you want to succeed in politics you must learn to keep your conscience under control. (David Lloyd George)

One lesson you'd better learn if you want to be in politics is: Never go out on a golf course and beat the president. (Lyndon B. Johnson)

You don't have to fool all the people all the time in politics, just enough to get elected. (Gerald Barzan)

I have half a mind to go into politics. I'm told that's all I'll need. (Tom Gilbert)

Don't vote. The government always gets in. (David McSavage)

Polygamy

Marrying a man who's been married before is a good idea from an ecological point of view. In a world where there are more women than men it makes sense to recycle. (Rita Rudner)

A woman should marry for love, and keep on marrying until she finds it. (Zsa Zsa Gabor)

The Pope

Don't take advice from the Pope about sex. If he knows anything about it, he shouldn't. (George Bernard Shaw)

The Pope should wear underpants in the bath so he doesn't have to look down on the unemployed. (Hal Holbrook)

Positive Thinking

My mom always said, 'Keep your chin up.' That's how I ran into the door. (Daryl Hogue)

I saw a book on positive thinking in a shop the other day. I was going to buy it but then I thought: What the hell good is *that* going to do me? (Ronnie Shakes)

Posterity

Why should we do anything for posterity? What's posterity ever done for us? (Sir Boyle Roche)

Postmen

The postman always rings twice. So don't answer him the first time. (Jimmy Cricket)

Posture

Don't do anything standing that can be done sitting or anything sitting that can be done lying down. (H.L. Mencken)

Practically anything you say will sound amusing if you're on all fours. (Auberon Waugh)

If you can't stand sex, try it lying down. (Peter Sellers)

Keep your eye on the ball, your nose to the grindstone and your shoulder to the wheel. But remember it's very difficult to work from that position. (Bob Monkhouse)

Potholing

Don't go potholing in Bogota without your shovel. (Adrian Higgins)

Power

There's only one way to leave power and that's kicking and screaming. (P.J. Mara)

Praise

Try praising your wife even if you're on the verge of divorce. The shock might kill her. (Stan Stenson)

Pre-Marital Sex

Sex before marriage is a good idea. Mainly because there's so little of it after it. (Brendan O'Carroll)

Sex before marriage is never to be recommended. It delays the ceremony. (Leonard Rossiter)

Prepositions

A preposition is something you should never end a sentence with. (Jill Etherington)

Presents

The best way to approach a girl with a past is with a present. (Hal Roach)

Prime Ministers

Every Prime minister needs a Willie. (Margaret Thatcher on Lord William Whitelaw)

Principles

Always remember : The most useful thing about a principle is that it can always be sacrificed to expediency. (W. Somerset Maugham)

Priorities

First things first. Second things never. (Shirley Conran)

Don't sweat the petty things. And don't pet the sweaty things. (Jay Leno)

Prison

If you're sentenced to death, the best way to save your life is to die in prison. (Tony Butler)

Prisoners of War

POWs should never address their captors by their first names. Neither should they ask them for any special favours at the weekend, like for instance the latest DVDs. (Harry Secombe)

Problems

Never complain about your problems. Do something about them instead. Run away from them. (Richard Pryor)

Don't tell your friends your problems. Your enemies will enjoy them much more. (Lenny Bruce)

The only way to solve a problem with a woman is to jump on her. Then things will work out. (Lee Marvin)

Procrastination

Never put off till tomorrow what you can do the day after. (Mark Twain)

My mom always told me never to put off till tomorrow people you can kill today. (Dennis Quaid in *Wyatt Earp*)

My mother said, 'You'll never amount to anything because you procrastinate.' I said, 'Just wait.' (Judy Tenuta)

Procrastinate now! (Graffiti)

Professionals

Always listen to the professionals and then do the opposite of what they say. (H.L. Mencken)

Promises

Never make a promise you can't break. (Gene Kerrigan)

Pronunciation

Never trust an Englishman who speaks French with the correct pronunciation. (Andre Maurois)

Never do anything in bed you can't pronounce. (Mitch Murray)

Proposals

Once a week is quite enough to propose marriage to anyone. (Oscar Wilde)

Prosperity

A couple of years ago mother told me, 'Sweetheart, settle down and marry a rich man.' I said, 'Mom, I *am* a rich man.' (Cher)

It's easier to make your second million than your first. So start with the second one. (Barbara Peyton)

Psychiatrists

One should only see a psychiatrist out of boredom. (Muriel Spark)

Anyone who sees a psychiatrist ought to have his head examined. (Sam Goldwyn)

How many psychiatrists does it take to change a lightbulb? Only one, but the bulb must *want* to be changed. (Sian Mitchell)

The Public

What the public criticises in you, cultivate. (Jean Cocteau)

Publicity

It's better to have loved and divorced than never to have had any publicity at all. (Ava Gardner)

Publishing

Publish and be sued. (Richard Ingrams)

Pubs

The best way to cross Dublin without passing a pub is to go into all of them. (James Joyce)

Do Not Leave Your Seat While The Bar Is In Motion. (Sign in pub)

Punching

The best advice my father ever gave me when I was young was, 'If you stop punching your sister, she'll let go of your hair.' (Terry Firth)

Punctuality

Better never than late. (George Bernard Shaw)

If you're there before it's over you're on time. (Niall Toibin)

The trouble with being punctual is that there's nobody there to appreciate it. (Des Bishop)

To ensure immediate arrival of breakfast in hotels, lock the door, remove your cloths and go into the lavatory. (Kenneth Tynan)

Prunes

Start a movement. Eat a prune. (Dick Van Dyke)

Puppy Love

Be wary of puppy love. It can lead to a dog's life. (Gladiola Montana)

Pyjamas

If you've been abusing your wife it's probably best to wear fire-resistant pyjamas to bed. (Michael Moore)

Never let a child wearing Superman pyjamas sleep on the top bunk. (Milton Berle)

Q

Queens

Treat every queen like a whore and every whore like a queen.
(Anthony Quinn)

Questions

If you need time to think about a question, make the questioner ask
it again. Then pretend you don't understand it. (W.B. O'Carolan)

Queues

If you ever see me in a queue at the railway booking office, join the
other one. Because there'll be a chap in front of me who's trying to
send a rhinoceros to Tokyo. (Basil Boothroyd)

Quotes

When in doubt, ascribe all quotations to George Bernard Shaw.
(Nigel Rees)

R

Racism

Racism is a terrible thing. We should all learn to hate one another on an individual basis. (Cathy Ladman)

Rain

Do not, on a rainy day, ask your child what he feels like doing. Because I assure you that what he feels like doing you will not feel like watching. (Fran Lebowitz)

Rashes

My albums are hard to swallow. If rash develops, discontinue use and consult your physician immediately. (Tom Waits)

Rattlesnakes

A rattlesnake that doesn't bite you teaches you nothing. (Jessamyn West)

Reading

Don't read science fiction books. It'll look bad if you die in bed with one on the nightstand. Always read stuff that will make you look good if you die in the middle of the night. (P.J. O'Rourke)

If you read that drinking is bad for you, give up reading. (Henny Youngman)

Reading Tolkien is okay as long as you don't get into the Hobbit. (Bill Campbell)

If you want to read about love and marriage, buy two separate books. (Alan King)

There's nothing like going to bed with a book. Or a friend who's read one. (Phyllis Diller)

You should always go to bed with a Trollop. (John Major)

Reality

Do not adjust your mind. Reality is at fault. (Bernard O'Shea)

Reality is just a crutch for people who can't cope with drugs. (Lily Tomlin)

Recession

Always look on the bright side of a recession. When you don't have any money you can't waste it. (David Miller)

What shall it profit a man if he gains the whole world and there's a recession? (Mel Brooks)

References

Never accept a reference from a clergyman. They always want to give someone a second chance. (Arnold Bennett)

Refusals

Learn to say no. It will be of more use to you than to be able to read Latin. (Charles Spurgeon)

Start by saying no to requests. Then if you have to go to yes, okay. But if you start with yes you can't go to no. (Mildred Perlman)

Regrets

Mum and Dad are dead now. I often think of some of the advice I wish I'd given them. Like, 'Be careful of that bus.' (Kevin Gildea)

Relatives

Get born without relatives if you can. (Henry Lawson)

Don't be too hard on your relatives. It's not their fault either. (Jasper Carrott)

Einstein is famous for his theory of relativity. I have my own one: Don't hire your relatives. (Sam Goldwyn)

Relaxation

We should all learn to take things easy – especially other people's things. (Harry Graham)

Religion

Religion is the best cure we have for violence in the world. A man fired a bullet at me once. My life was saved by a copy of The Bible I was carrying in my hand at the time. (Herb Caen)

Repairs

If it's not baroque, don't fix it. (Linda Wolverton)

Repetition

When you're telling your children something, first you have to tell them you're going to tell them. Then you tell them. Then you tell them you've told them. And then they forget it. (Jimmy Hutchins)

You can't repeat the first time of something. (Christina Aguilera)

Reputations

If you want to injure someone's reputation don't speak ill of them but too well. (Andre Siegfried)

Until you've lost your reputation you never really realise what a burden it is. (Margaret Mitchell)

Restaurants

Never eat in a restaurant where antacid is lidted on the menu as a side dish. (Gene Perret)

Never recommend a restaurant to anyone. Something always goes wrong with the cheese *soufflé*. (Edmond Love)

Retirement

Life is all about preparation. Before you retire, stay home for a week and watch daytime television. (Fred Metcalf)

When a colleague retires it's not considered good form to snatch a chair while he's still in it. (Lynne Alpern)

Revenge

When a man steals your wife, there's no better revenge than to let him keep her. (Sacha Guitry)

If a man lies to you, don't get mad, get even. I once dated a guy who waited three months into our relationship before telling me he was married. I said, 'Hey, don't worry about it. I used to be a man.' (Livia Squires)

Rings

Never give back the ring. Never. Swallow it first. (Joan Rivers)

Always give back the ring but keep the stone. (Zsa Zsa Gabor)

Rivals

If you can't beat 'em, join 'em. Then arrange to have 'em beaten. (Will Rogers)

Road Maps

If you're driving from London to Athens, be aware that the most challenging part of the journey will be trying to fold the road map and fit it snugly in the glove compartment. (Gary Hansard)

Rome

When in Rome, do as the Greeks. (Denis Donoghue)

When in Rome, stay there. (John Huston)

Rubik's Cube

Rubik's Cube cures sanity. (Dave Henderson)

Rules

Don't learn the rules. Then you can't be accused of breaking them. (Mary Robinson)

Rumours

Don't believe any false rumours until you hear them from me. (Vic Schiro)

Safe Cross Code

Practise a new version of the Safe Cross Code by crossing crowded motorways at rush hour. This will sharpen your reflexes. If a car hits you and you get sent to hospital, the experience will test your ability to withstand agonising pain. If you die, try to move faster the next time. (Bill Hicks)

Safe Sex

I don't think safe sex is a good idea. Who wants sex in a safe? (Steve Martin)

Safe sex is very important. That's why I'm never going to do it on plywood scaffolding again. (Jenny Jones)

Practise safe sex. Fuck yourself. (Andy Kaufman)

Sales

The important thing in selling is to make the customer think he's getting laid when he's getting fucked. (Michael Bloomberg)

Scandals

Don't make your debut in life with a scandal. Reserve it to give an interest to your old age. (Oscar Wilde)

Schizophrenics

Never tell depressed schizophrenics to pull themselves together. (Mort Sahl)

My psychiatrist told me to be myself. That's difficult when you have multiple personalities. (Phil Tully)

Schizophrenics should be at two with nature. (Woody Allen)

If you're a psychiatrist dealing with a pair of Siamese twins suffering from schizophrenia, charge quadruple. (Frank Carson)

Seasickness

The best cure for seasickness is to sit under a tree. (Spike Milligan)

Seating

If you're having people over for the evening, never sit interesting ones with bores. Put all the bores at one table. They don't know they're bores and they'll all have a wonderful time. (Joyce Haber)

If the person sitting next to you in the theatre dies during a play, move to the next seat. (Quentin Crisp)

Secrets

If you want the secret of my success with women, don't smoke, don't take drugs and don't be too particular. (George Best)

To have a happy marriage tell your spouse everything except the essentials. (Cynthia Nelms)

Self-Belief

You've got to believe in yourself if you're going to win something. I always believe England will win the World Cup right up to the moment the referee blows the final whistle and we're knocked out. (Peter Shilton)

Self-Defence

Never raise a hand to your children. It leaves your mid-section unprotected. (Robert Orpen)

Sex

Sex is a wonderful thing between two people – if you can get between the right two people. (Woody Allen)

If you want your girlfriend to scream when you're having sex, for heaven's sake ring her up and tell her. (Ivor Dembina)

Casual sex is best because you don't have to wear a tie. (John Mendoza)

My mother and I had different attitudes to sex. She said, 'Never sleep with a man until he buys you a house.' It worked for her. I ended up with a swing out back. (Judy Brown)

Never have sex with any woman who doesn't respect your wife. (Billy Crystal)

Don't have sex. It leads to kissing, and pretty soon you have to talk to them. (Steve Martin)

Shoes

Here's a useful shopping tip. You can get a pair of shoes for £1 at bowling alleys. (Al Clethen)

If you want to confuse a girl, buy her a pair of chocolate shoes. (Milton Jones)

If the shoe fits, buy it in every available colour. (Imelda Marcos)

Shopping

Whoever said money can't buy happiness obviously isn't shopping at the right places. (Wendy Hiller)

Shopping is better than sex because it's easier to exchange. (Adrienne Gusoff)

If you send a man out to buy eggs and sugar in the supermarket, don't be surprised if he comes home with a case of wine, a pair of jeans and a tree. (Helen Rowland)

Shooting

Always shoot to kill. Dead men can't grass on you. (Ronnie Kray)

They should shoot more actors and less movies. (Walter Winchell)

Shouting

Don't shout for help at night. You might wake the neighbours. (Stanislaus Lec)

Sincerity

Always be sincere whether you mean it or not. (Fred Allen)

Singles Bars

There's only one good reason to go to a singles bar these days: to meet someone who's married. (Dave Allen)

Sinks

Love begins when you sink in his arms. It ends with your arms in his sink. (Eleanor Parker)

Sins

Commit the oldest sins in the newest kind of way. (William Shakespeare)

Christ died for our sins. Dare we make his martyrdom meaningless by not committing them? (Jules Feiffer)

Once a woman has forgiven her man she shouldn't re-heat his sins for breakfast. (Marlene Dietrich)

Skeletons

If you can't get rid of the family skeleton you may as well make it dance. (George Bernard Shaw)

Slander

Never badmouth your ex-husband to your kids. If you do you'll ruin the moment when they figure it out for themselves. (Cozy Kahoney)

Sleep

Try to get as much sleep as you can. Most of the bad things people do in their lives are when they're awake. (James Simpson)

Sleep with a public servant. He needs the exercise. (Julie Birchill)

Nurses should never forget to wake patients up to take their sleeping pills. (Marion Collery)

Sleep is an excellent way of listening to an opera. (James Stephens)

I say to my children, 'Sleep with anyone you like but don't beget children.' That's my morality. (Edna O'Brien)

He sleepeth fastest who sleepeth alone. (Richard Avedon)

Sleeping Pills

Never under any circumstances take a sleeping pill and a laxative on the same night . (Dave Barry)

Smartness

If you want to be considered smart, agree with everyone. (Leo Rosten)

A smart girl is one who knows how to play tennis, golf, piano...and dumb. (Marilyn Monroe)

Smells

Avoid smells in the kitchen. Don't cook. (Bette Midler)

Put kitty litter in your shoes and it will take away the odour. Unless you own a cat. (Jay Leno)

Smiles

Start the day with a smile and get it over with. (Les Dawson)

Smile – it confuses people. (Scott Adams)

Always keep a smile on your face. It would look ridiculous anywhere else. (Marty Feldman)

Smoking

Here's a tip to stop smoking. Douse yourself in petrol every day. (Bill Bailey)

Stop smoking. Carry wet matches. (Bob Monkhouse)

Smoking kills. If you're killed you've lost a very important part of your life. (Brooke Shields)

Smokers: Save pounds every year on matches and cigarette lighters by lighting your cigarette with the butt of the previous one. (*Viz*)

I agree that passive smoking is outrageous. They should pay for their own. (Rhona Cameron)

The doctor told me to do something that puts me out of breath so I've taken up smoking again. (Jo Brand)

Don't smoke. It shortens your cigarettes. (Bernard Manning)

Sneezing

You can sometimes bring reluctant sneezes on by staring into lights. Don't do this when you're driving. You may get a satisfying sneeze but it will be your last one. (Guy Browning)

Snooker

I think it's a great idea to talk during sex, as long as it's about snooker. (Steve Davis)

Snoring

Laugh and the world laughs with you. Snore and you sleep alone. (Herb Caen)

Cure your snoring habit: Stay awake all night. (Leopold Fechtner)

Snow

Before you love, learn to run through snow leaving no footprints. (Turkish proverb)

The best way to stop snow sticking to your shovel is to move to Florida. (Leopold Fechtner)

Sobriety

Better to sleep with a sober cannibal than a drunken Christian. (Herman Melville)

Sobriety should only be practised in moderation. (John Ciardi)

You should always be sober enough to know when you're drunk. (Dylan Thomas)

My father once told me that if you haven't had a drink in weeks and five intelligent people look at you and tell you you're dead drunk, the best thing to do is not to argue but to lie down and take a nap for an hour. (Joseph Schenck)

Social Workers

Help a child. Kill a social worker. (Alexei Sayle)

Socialising

My wife said we should get out more. Now we'll never see one another. (Chevy Chase)

Socks

How do you know if your socks need washing? Throw them at the ceiling. If they stay up there they do. (Brendan Behan)

My idea of a colour-coordinated wardrobe is matching socks. (Jim Royle)

The best way to get rid of a hole in your sock is to turn it inside out. (Jack Cruise)

Don't wear socks. Then when people tell you to pull them up, you can't. (Jeffrey Barnard)

The best stocking filler? A leg. (Norm McDonald)

Soho

Anything goes in Soho. Just make sure it's not your wallet. (Jo Brand)

Soldiers

When I was a soldier I was taught, 'If it moves, salute it. If not, whitewash it.' (Anthony Burgess)

Solitude

If Greta Garbo really wanted to be left alone she should have come to a screening of one of her films in Dublin. (Hugh Leonard)

It is not good for man to be alone. But oh, what a relief. (John Barrymore)

Sows

You can't make a silk purse out of a sow's ear but there's nothing to stop you making a lovely pork pie out of one. (Humphrey Lyttleton)

You could cover a sow's ear with silk purses but the damn bristles would still work their way through. (Marie Lloyd)

Space

If the man in your life tells you he wants space, put him out in the garden. There's lots of it there. (Roseanne)

Space Travel

If Richard Branson has persuaded you to become a space tourist and journey with him to Jupiter, make sure you bring a good book. (Ellen Quaid)

Never send a dog up in a space shuttle. On re-entry it will stick its head out the window and be burnt up. (Rory Byrne)

If you're planning on going to the sun, go up at night and it won't burn you. (Jack O'Leary)

They've put a man on the moon. Now let's get the rest of them up there. (Kathy Lette)

Spaghetti

The best way to keep the rice from sticking when you make spaghetti is to boil each grain separately. (Annette Temple)

Speculation

There are two times in your life when you shouldn't speculate. When you can't afford it and when you can. (Mark Twain)

Speeches

The speeches to be wary of are those that begin, 'I'm just going to say a few words.' (Frank Muir)

Anytime a speechmaker says, 'Long story short', say, 'Too late!' Because it always is. (Robert Morley)

My father gave me three hints about speech-making: Be sincere, be brief, be seated. (James Roosevelt)

Speed

Speed kills. Die happy. (Joel Redmond)

Spellers

Bad speller of the world untie. (Frankie Boyle)

Spitting

Never spit in a man's face unless his moustache is on fire. (Henry Root)

Spoons

There's always a spoon left in the sink after you wash the dishes so next time don't put one in. Use a fork to stir your tea instead. (Doug Sanders)

Squirrels

Preserve wild life. Pickle a squirrel. (Jasper Carrott)

Stability

If you stand still there's only one way you can go. Backwards. (Peter Shilton)

If you can keep your head when all about you are losing theirs you probably don't understand the problem. (Jean Kerr)

If you can keep your head when all about you are losing theirs you'll be taller than everyone else. (Steve Allen)

Stag Nights

It doesn't really matter what you do on your stag night as long as you wake up naked the next morning handcuffed to an orang-utan in the hold of a Boeing 707 which has just landed in Jakarta. (Adrian Edmondson)

Stairs

Don't stare up the steps. Step up the stairs. (Bertrand Russell)

Stalkers

If you're being stalked by an angry mob with raspberries, the first thing to do is release a tiger. (John Cleese)

Stand-Up Comedians

My advice to stand-up comedians? Wear a pair of brown trousers. (Jasper Carrott)

Never do a gig in a place where they still point at aeroplanes. (Frank Skinner)

Stigmas

Any stigma is good enough to beat a dogma with. (Philip Guadella)

Stockbrokers

Never trust a stockbroker who's married to a travel agent. (Ed Weldon)

Stomachs

I wouldn't advise anyone to use Napoleon's advice about an army marching on its stomach. They wouldn't get very far from that position. (Gwen Pollard)

Stomach pains can often be caused by eating nothing on an empty stomach. (Seamus O'Sullivan)

They say the way to a man's heart is through his stomach. Personally I'd go a bit lower. (Roseanne)

The way to a man's heart may be through his stomach but that's only if you twist the blade and lift it up. (Sheila Kay)

Storms

Before a storm brews in a teacup, nip it in the bud. (Russell Grant)

Strangers

When I was ten my father told me not to talk to strangers. We haven't spoken since. (Steven Wright)

Don't talk to strangers unless you know them. (Kenneth Grahame)

Strippers

Don't just stand there, undo something. (Bob Hope to Gypsy Rose Lee)

If you're looking for a way to piss your mother off, stop your car in front of the local strip joint and say, 'I'll be right back. I just have to run in and pick up my cheque.' (Judy Gold)

Subsistence

Live within your means even if you have to borrow to do so. (Artemis Ward)

Success

My formula for success is: Rise early, work late and strike oil. (J. Paul Getty)

The only way to succeed is to make people hate you. That way they remember you. (Joseph von Sternberg)

If A is success, then A equals X plus Y plus Z. Work is X, Y is play and Z is keeping your mouth shut. (Albert Einstein)

Suckers

Never give a sucker a lollipop. (W.C. Fields)

Sugar

A spoonful of sugar helps the medicine go down. Two spoonfuls work even better. And better again if you don't bother with the medicine. (Jack Lemmon)

Suicide

Guns are best for suicide. They're more stylish-looking than razor blades. And of course gas has gotten so expensive. Drugs aren't good either. They're too chancy. You might miscalculate the dosage and just have a good time. (P.J. O'Rourke)

I think assisted suicide should be legal. Especially if the person you're assisting has a rent-controlled apartment. (Janine DiTullio)

If the Samaritans hang up on you in the middle of a suicide attempt it might be a sign that you need to brush up on your social skills. (Aidan O'Shea)

Don't commit suicide while you're drunk or you might regret it when you sober up. (Dean Martin)

Don't kill yourself. Go to Belgium instead. (Stephen Fry)

Suicide Bombers

Rules for conversing with a suicide bomber: 1) Be polite but firm. 2) Resist the temptation to discuss your personal problems. (Simon Munnery)

Superstition

Don't be superstitious. It brings bad luck. (Neil Fleming)

Surgeons

Never allow yourself be operated on by a surgeon who has more than two plasters on his fingers. (Gene Lucaire)

Survival

Marry an outdoor woman. Then if you throw her out in the yard for the night she can still survive. (W.C. Fields)

Suspicion

Always suspect everybody. (Charles Dickens)

Swearing

Don't swear before your wife. Let her swear first. (Terry Cooper)

Do not take the lord's name in vain. Select a time when it will have an effect. (Ambrose Bierce)

Sympathy

Don't solicit sympathy. It's only a word in the dictionary between shit and syphilis. (Gene Wilder)

Table Tennis

Never play table tennis with your mouth open. (Leopold Fechtner)

Tactics

If Plan A fails, try Plan A. (Jack Charlton)

Talk Shows

There's only one unbreakable rule about talk shows: No jockeys. (Declan Lynch)

Tattoos

Never get a tattoo because if you turn to a life of crime you'll be easily recognisable. (Amy Lame)

Taxis

Don't grab a girl the moment you get into a taxi. Wait until the driver puts down the flag. (George Jean Nathan)

Tip a taxicab driver $40 in New York if he doesn't mention his haemorrhoids. (Dave Barry)

Always haggle with your taxi driver over the fare. He'll take pity on you for being poor and put you up in his home completely free of charge. (Adrian Edmondson)

Tea

The best thing to do after you see your dead husband's body on the floor is to have a cup of tea. (Anthony Burgess)

Tea Cosies

Never trust a man who, when he's alone in a room with a tea cosy, doesn't try it on. (Billy Connolly)

Teenagers

Remember that as a teenager you're at the last stage of your life when you'll be happy to hear the phone is for you. (Fran Lebowitz)

Teenagers should leave home while they still know everything. (Bill Cosby)

Teeth

Be true to your teeth lest they be false to you. (Derek Roy)

You have to take the bull by the teeth. (Sam Goldwyn)

Never fight anyone who has worse teeth than you have. You have too much to lose. (Mel Brooks)

The doctor told me to stop grinding my teeth. Now before I go to sleep I fill my mouth with hot water and coffee beans and set the alarm for 7.30. (Jeff Marder)

Say no to yellow teeth. Having them colour coordinated with fading hair isn't much of a turn-on. (Michael Shea)

One of the major disadvantages of sleeping with someone on a regular basis is that you end up doing your teeth at exactly the same time. This means you find yourself turning the tap on and off 500 times, headbutting each other and spitting great jollops of toothpaste on the back of each other's head. This often leads to a demand for separate bathrooms, separate bedrooms and finally separate lives. (Guy Browning)

I finally have a dental plan I can afford. I chew on the other side. (Janine DiTullio)

Television

Never buy a portable TV set in the street from a man who's out of breath. (Arnold Glasgow)

Why pay to go out and see a lousy film in the cinema when you can stay home and watch a lousy TV programme for nothing? (Sam Goldwyn)

Sex on the television isn't to be recommended. You might fall off. (Sue Lyons)

Temperature

Be suspicious of any doctor who tries to take your temperature with his finger. (David Letterman)

Temptation

The best way to get rid of temptation is to yield to it. (Clementina Graham)

Don't worry about avoiding temptation. As you get older it will avoid you. (Joey Adams)

Lord, lead us not into temptation. Just tell me where it is and I'll find it myself. (Rita Mae Brown)

Tennis

If you're up against a girl with big boobs, bring her to the net and make her hit backhand volleys. (Billy Jean King)

There's only one rule you need to follow in mixed doubles: Always aim for the girl. (Ilie Nastase)

Tequila

One tequila, two tequila, three tequila, floor. (George Carlin)

Testicles

If it has tyres or testicles you'll have trouble with it. (Linda Furney)

Never trust a man with testicles. (Jo Brand)

Theft

My grandfather always said, 'Don't watch your money, watch your health.' But one day while I was watching my health, someone stole my money. It was my grandfather. (Jackie Mason)

Throats

I have a perfect cure for a sore throat. Cut it. (Alfred Hitchcock)

Thumbs

Don't suck your thumb. Or anyone else's. (Forrest Gump)

Time

There's no time like the pleasant. (Addison Mizner)

Time may be a great healer but it's a lousy beautician. (Lucille Harper)

There comes a time in everyone's life when he must make way for an older man. (Reginald Maudling)

Time is the best teacher. Unfortunately, it kills all the students. (Franklin P. Jones)

Life is a waste of time and time is a waste of life so get wasted all the time and have the time of your life. (Michelle Mastrolacasa)

Timing

There comes a tide in the affairs of men which, taken at the flood, leads absolutely nowhere. (Emo Philips)

Toads

Eat a live toad first thing in the morning and be guaranteed nothing worse will happen to you all day. (Renee Mercer)

Toasters

A good present for your girlfriend is a toaster but don't give it to her while she's in the bath, especially if it's plugged in at the time. It makes the toast all soggy. (John Belushi)

Toilet Training

Modern parents believe toilet training should be an easy and casual affair. Parents who are even more modern just let their son shit over everything. This prepares him to be a brilliant conversationalist later in life. (P.J. O'Rourke)

Toilets

I advised my wife to buy a toilet brush for the bathroom but she didn't like it. We're back to using paper again now. (Tommy Cooper)

In a public toilet, incoming traffic should have the right of way. (Hugh Leonard)

Toilet damaged. Use floor below. (Notice in pub toilet)

Toys

Never buy a toy that says 'Easy to Assemble.' A few hours later you will undoubtedly find yourself in a straitjacket. (Robert Morley)

Tradition

If people keep pushing tradition at you about your impending marriage, tell them you've decided tto adopt the ancient one of the Aztecs where they sacrificed the bride's family's first-born son and ate his liver off the wedding altar. (Peter Downey)

Trains

The best way to catch a train is to miss the one before it. (G.K. Chesterton)

If you board the wrong train it's no good running along the corridor in the other direction. (Dietrich Bonhoeffer)

Transsexuals

If you have to ask if somebody is male or female, don't. (Patrick Murray)

The happiest kind of man is one who wants to eat, drink and be Mary. (Lily Savage)

Travel

Don't go to Australia. It's already tomorrow over there so they'll know if something terrible is going to happen to you. (Clive James)

Trouble

A trouble shared is a trouble doubled. (Marian Keyes)

If you help someone when they're in trouble they'll remember it...the next time they're in trouble. (Orson Welles)

Trousers

Never wear your best trousers when you go out to fight for truth and freedom. (Henrik Ibsen)

Trousers may now be worn by ladies on the golf course but they must be removed upon entering the clubhouse. (Notice)

Only attempt to take your trousers off over your head if you've been drinking Southern Comfort. (Bill Carson)

Trust

Don't trust a man unless you've got his pecker in your pocket. (Lyndon B. Johnson)

Never trust a thin cook. (Charlotte Wright)

Never trust anyone who listens to Mahler before they're forty. (Clive James)

Never trust anyone who wears a beard, a bow tie, two-toned shoes or sunglasses. (Michael Caine)

Trust everyone, but cut the cards. (Finley Peter Dunne)

Truth

Truth is the most valuable thing we have. Therefore let us be sparing in its use. (Claud Cockburn)

When you tell the truth, have one foot in the stirrup. (Kinky Friedman)

It's always best to tell the truth. Unless, of course, one is an exceptionally good liar. (Jerome K. Jerome)

Be truthful to everyone except the cops and the woman in your life. (Jack Nicholson)

Tell the truth and shame the family. (Ethel Watts Mumford)

U

Ulcers

Don't get ulcers, give 'em. (Ed Koch)

Umbrellas

A businessman needs three umbrellas: One to have at the office, one to have at home and one to leave on the train. (Paul Dickson)

Underestimation

Never underestimate a man who overestimates himself. (Franklin D. Roosevelt)

Never underestimate a child's ability to get into even more trouble. (Martin Mull)

Don't mis-underestimate me. (George Bush)

Unemployment

One of the best ways to pass the time if you're unemployed is to iron your socks. (Brush Sheils)

I've found a solution to unemployment. Raise the school-leaving age to 65. (Sean McDonnell)

Unfulfilment

Better murder an infant in its cradle than nurse an unacted desire. (William Blake)

Unification

Eggheads of the world unite. You have nothing to lose but your yolks. (Adlai Stevenson)

Free Northern Ireland. Sign a partition. (Patrick Kielty)

The best way to get the Beatles together again is to shoot the remaining two. (Jonas Sheidlin)

Urination

Cut out the middle man. Pee into the Thames. (Nigel Rees)

If you're able to read this you're aiming in the wrong direction. (Sign in urinal)

Don't drink too much beer. It could be the urination of you. (Kingsley Amis)

Used Cars

Only buy a used car when it's new. (David Kinnell)

When buying a used car, punch the buttons on the radio. If all the stations are rock 'n roll there's a good chance the transmission is shot. (Larry Lujac)

V

Vampires

I've always thought becoming a vampire was a good idea. You'd save a fortune on sun cream. (Frankie Howerd)

If you're going drinking with a vampire, stay away from Bloody Marys. (Denise Staunton)

Vandalism

Stamp out vandalism or I'll break your windows. (Johnny Rotten)

Variety

Variety may be the spice of life but it's monotony that buys the groceries. (Michael Shea)

The best way to kill a variety act is to go for the juggler. (Jim Davidson)

Varnish

Drink varnish. It's a terrible end but a lovely finish. (Bill Coates)

Vegetables

All vegetables should be boiled for at least a month before a dinner in case one of the guests turns up without his teeth. (Calvin Trillin)

Viagra

If you're not mad for sex, marry an older type of man who thinks Viagra is a waterfall. (Emma Bunton)

Viagra for everyone. Then we'd all be able to get it over the counter. (Roy Braberton)

Vices

Never trust a man who hasn't any redeeming vices. (Winston Churchill)

If you're stuck between two vices, choose an original one. (Tallulah Bankhead)

Videos

If you're unhappily married, re-play the video of your wedding so that it ends with you and your betrothed arriving at the church from opposite directions. (Bob Monkhouse)

Vigilance

While your friend holds you affectionately by both of your hands you're safe. Because you can then watch both of his. (Ambrose Bierce)

Violence

Don't hit a man while he's down. He might get up and hit you back. (Danny Cummins)

Never hit anyone below the belt – especially if he's wearing a karate one. (Fred Allen)

We should get violence off the streets and into the churches where it belongs. (Jonathan Miller)

Certain women should be struck regularly, like gongs. (Noel Coward)

Virgin Airlines

It's not a good idea to fly with Virgin. Why use an airline that doesn't go all the way? (Dinny Moran)

Vocabulary

Learn to speak proper. (Pat Spillane)

'Always' and 'never' are two words you should always remember never to use. (Wendell Johnson)

Volleyball

The main purpose of volleyball is to get your sexual parts to flop around. It isn't much good unless played in the nude. (P.J. O'Rourke)

Vomiting

Vomiting is one of the best ways to get clothes to fit you. (Jo Brand)

Enya is an effective emetic and is responsible for acute episodes of nausea, vomiting and diarrhoea. If you want to lose weight, put her CDs on now. (David Slattery)

Voting

Don't vote. The government always gets in. (Jack Cruise)

Voyeurism

Peeping Toms are advised to pull down their drapes when I undress. (Phyllis Diller)

W

Walking

In a dangerous neighbourhood always walk backwards so no one can sneak up on you. It also cuts down on the risk of stubbing your toe. (Barry Blyveis)

War

Make love, not war. Or get married and do both. (Greg Knight)

Make war, not love – it's safer. (Zero Mostel)

No bastard ever won a war by dying for his country. He won it by making the other bastard die for his one. (General George Patton)

War Films

If you're appearing in a war film, never share a foxhole with a character who carries a photo of his sweetheart in his wallet. (Del Close)

Warnings

Tobacco and alcohol warnings are too general. They should be more to the point: 'People who smoke will eventually throw up small brown pieces of lung.' Or, 'Warning. Alcohol will turn you into the same asshole your father was.' (George Carlin)

Water

Don't drink water. Fish fuck in it. (W.C. Fields)

Waving

If you're on stage and your flies are undone, wave. It distracts people. (Peter O'Toole)

Weapons

I'm all in favour of keeping dangerous weapons out of the hands of fools. Let's start with typewriters. (Thomas Berger)

Weddings

Be a bitch at your wedding. Suddenly pretend to go into labour as you walk down the aisle. (Pamela Stephenson)

It's a bad idea to get too drunk at a wedding. Especially if you're performing it. (Phil Silvers)

If it wasn't for the presents, an elopement would be preferable. (George Ade)

Wedding Dresses

You should skimp on your wedding dress. Why pay a lot of money for something you're only going to wear five or six times? (Charisse Chavarin)

Weight

Always be weary of anything that weighs less than its operating manual. (Terry Prachett)

It's no good tiptoeing to the bathroom scales. They can hear you coming. (Pam Brown)

Werewolves

Never moon a werewolf. (Mike Binder)

Whales

Save the whales. Collect the whole set. (Steven Wright)

Whistling

Never take a cross-country trip with a kid who's just learned to whistle. (Jean Deuel)

Whores

The best way to make a hormone? Don't pay her. (Bob Monkhouse)

Whorehouses

Wherever you go, especially if you're in a strange town, always find yourself a good whorehouse to stay at. They invariably serve the best breakfasts. When a staff has been working all night, it stands to reason they'll be very hungry. Arthur Caesar)

Too many cocks spoil the brothel. (Joe Orton)

Wives

Every man should have a wife – preferably his own. (Britt Ekland)

Better to be without a wife for a year than without tobacco for an hour. (Estonian proverb)

My notion of a wife at forty is that a man should be able to change her, like a banknote, for two twenties. (Douglas Jerrold)

Never tell your wife she's lousy in bed. She'll go out and get a second opinion. (Rodney Dangerfield)

Windows

When you're cleaning your windows, just do the insides. That means you'll be able to see out but the neighbours won't be able to see in. (Tommy Cooper)

Windscreens

If a bird craps on your windscreen, don't ask her out again. (Jim Davidson)

Windsurfing

Never practise windsurfing in an elevator even if the weather is clement. (Claire Thompson)

Wine

Use wine when you cook. Even put it in the food now and again. (Chevy Chase)

Don't serve red wine in your home unless you really hate your furniture. (Jean Gonick)

A glass of wine a day, we're told, cuts the risk of a stroke in half. Imagine what two would do? With three or four you might make a pass at your sister-in-law. Okay, that's not nice behaviour but at least you wouldn't get a stroke doing it. (Tommy Tiernan)

Winning

Winning doesn't really matter as long as you win. (Vinnie Jones)

Wires

Any wire cut to exactly the right length will be too short. (Arthur Bloch)

Wisdom

It's easy to be wise. Just think of something stupid to say and don't say it. (Sam Levinson)

Women

Women should be obscene and not heard. (John Lennon)

Treat every woman as if you've slept with her and you soon will. (Duc de la Rochefoucauld)

The surest way to a woman's heart is to aim kneeling. (Douglas Jerrold)

Don't give women advice. One should never give a woman anything she can't wear in the evening. (Oscar Wilde)

A woman should behave like a cook in the kitchen and a whore in the bedroom. (Oliver Reed)

It would be more fun if she behaved like a whore in the kitchen and a cook in the bedroom. (Groucho Marx)

Women's Ages

If you want to know how old a woman is, ask her sister-in-law. (Woody Allen)

Never trust a woman who tells you her real age. A woman who tells you that will tell you anything. (Oscar Wilde)

Women's Clubs

My advice to the women's clubs of America is: Raise more hell and less dahlias. (James McNeil Whistler)

Women's Liberation

Beware of the man who praises Women's Lib. He is about to leave his job. (Erica Jong)

Wool

If you want to pull the wool over a woman's eyes you need a good yarn. (Gyles Brandreth)

Work

Being busy is the best excuse for not working. (Kenneth Tynan)

All work and no play makes Jack's wife a rich widow. (Tom McDermott)

Working Out

Don't bother working out. If God wanted us to bend over he'd have put diamonds on the floor. (Elizabeth Taylor)

My philosophy of working out is: no pain, no pain. (Carol Liefer)

World War 3

A good way to prevent World War 3 is to stay friends with anyone you know who has their finger on the nuclear button. Also, if you bring your dog for a walk, don't forget the pooper scooper. (Dudley Moore)

Wrinkles

The best way to prevent sagging as you grow older is to keep eating until the wrinkles fall out. (John Candy)

Worry

Worrying is the most natural and spontaneous of all human functions so we should learn to do it better. (Lewis Thomas)

Today is the tomorrow you worried about yesterday. Be innovative and worry about yesterday tomorrow. (Fred Allen)

Stop worrying about your health. It'll go away. (Robert Orpen)

Writing

If you want to get rich from writing, write the sort of thing that's read by people who move their lips when they're reading. (Don Marquis)

The only way to make money at writing is to marry a publisher's daughter. (John Hammond)

The only way to make money at writing is to write ransom notes. (Mickey Spillane)

Wrongdoing

If two wrongs don't make a right, try three. (Norman Cousins)

X

X-Rays

If you don't like your X-rays, ask the radiologist to 'doctor' them. (Joey Bishop)

Y

You and Others

Do unto others that which you want them to do unto you, only do it first. (George Cohen)

Do unto others that which you would have them do unto you only if you're a masochist. (Arthur Bloch)

Do not do unto others as you would have them do unto you. Their tastes may not be the same. (George Bernard Shaw)

Youth

It's better to waste one's youth than to do nothing with it at all. (Georges Courteline)

If you want to recapture your youth, cut off his allowance. (Al Bernstein)

I've always believed the secret of eternal youth is arrested development. (Alice Roosevelt Longworth)

The secret of eternal youth is to lie about one's age. (Bob Hope)

Z

Zoos

A petting zoo is a great place if you want your kid's clothes to end up inside a goat's stomach. (Bill Dwyer)

The important thing when visiting the zoo is not to be mistaken for one of the animals. If you are, they may not let you home. (Truman Capote)

Zumba Dancing

If you're suffering from diarrhoea, don't do any zumba dancing in tight trousers, especially after drinking cappucchino. (Albert Groom)